Saint
Paul
the Apostle

Saint
Paul
the Apostle

POPE
BENEDICT XVI

Our Sunday Visitor Publishing Division
Our Sunday Visitor, Inc.
Huntington, Indiana 46750

Copyright © 2009 by Libreria Editrice Vaticana

Copyright © 2009 by Our Sunday Visitor Publishing Division
Our Sunday Visitor, Inc.   Published 2009

14 13 12 11 10 09   1 2 3 4 5 6 7 8 9

ISBN 978-1-59276-615-4 (Inventory No. T897)
LCCN: 2009925561

Cover design by Tyler Ottinger
Interior design by Sherri L. Hoffman

Cover art: St. Paul
El Greco (1541–1614)
The Granger Collection, New York

PRINTED IN THE UNITED STATES OF AMERICA

CONTENTS

INTRODUCTION*†

The year 2008 saw the happy circumstance of the inauguration of the Pauline Year, which I desired to institute in order to commemorate the second millennium of St. Paul's birth, with the intention of promoting an ever deeper reflection on the theological and spiritual inheritance bequeathed to the Church by the Apostle to the Gentiles with his vast and profound work of evangelization.

St. Paul reminds us that full communion among all Christians is founded on "one Lord, one faith, one baptism" (Eph 4:5). May our common faith, the one Baptism for the forgiveness of sins and obedience to the one Lord and Savior, therefore, be fully expressed in the community and ecclesial dimensions as soon as possible. "One body and one Spirit," the Apostle to the Gentiles says, and he adds, "just as you were called to the one hope" (Eph 4:4). St. Paul also points out to us a reliable way to preserve unity, and in the case of division, to restore it. The Decree on Ecumenism of the Second Vatican Council took Paul's suggestion and represented it in the context of ecumenical commitment, referring to the rich and ever timely words of the Letter to the Ephesians: "I therefore, a prisoner for the Lord, beg you to walk

---

* Editor's Note: The material in this book is derived from catecheses given by Pope Benedict XVI during his weekly general audiences from July 2, 2008, through February 4, 2009. The texts have been edited only slightly to facilitate presentation in book form. The date each address was originally presented is annotated in the footnotes.

† Address of His Holiness Benedict XVI to His Holiness Bartholomew I, Ecumenical Patriarch, on the Occasion of the Solemnity of the Holy Apostles Peter and Paul for the Opening of the Pauline Year, June 28, 2008.

in a manner worthy of the calling to which you have been called, with all lowliness and meekness, with patience, forbearing one another in love, eager to maintain the unity of the Spirit in the bond of peace" (4:1–3).

St. Paul was not afraid to address a strong appeal to the Christians of Corinth among whom disputes had arisen, so that they might be unanimous in their speech, that the dissensions among them disappear and that they foster perfect union of thought and intention (cf. 1 Cor 1:10). In our world, in which the phenomenon of globalization is being consolidated but where divisions and conflicts continue to persist, men and women feel increasingly the need for certainties and peace. At the same time, however, they are bewildered and, as it were, enticed by a certain hedonistic and relativistic culture which casts doubt even on the existence of the truth. In this regard, the Apostle's instructions are particularly favorable for encouraging the efforts to seek full unity among all Christians, so necessary to offer the people of the third millennium an ever more luminous witness of Christ, the Way, the Truth, and the Life. Only in Christ and in his Gospel can humanity find a response to its deepest expectations.

May St. Paul help the Christian people to renew their ecumenical commitment and may our common initiatives on the way towards communion among all Christ's disciples be intensified.

CHAPTER ONE

Religious and Cultural Environment[*]

I began a cycle of catecheses focusing on the great Apostle St. Paul. The year was dedicated to him, from the liturgical Feast of Sts. Peter and Paul on June 29, 2008, to the same feast day in 2009. The Apostle Paul, an outstanding and almost inimitable yet stimulating figure, stands before us as an example of total dedication to the Lord and to his Church, as well as of great openness to humanity and its cultures. It is right, therefore, that we reserve a special place for him in not only our veneration but also in our effort to understand what he has to say to us as well, Christians of today. In this first chapter let us pause to consider the environment in which St. Paul lived and worked. A theme such as this would seem to bring us far from our time, given that we must identify with the world of 2,000 years ago. Yet this is only apparently and, in any case, only partly true, for we can see that various aspects of today's social and cultural context are not very different from what they were then.

A primary and fundamental fact to bear in mind is the relationship between the milieu in which Paul was born and raised and the global context to which he later belonged. He came from a very precise and circumscribed culture, indisputably a minority, which is that of the people of Israel and its tradition. In the ancient world, and especially in the Roman Empire, as scholars on the

---

[*] General Audience, July 2, 2008.

subject teach us, Jews must have accounted for about 10 percent of the total population; later, here in Rome, towards the middle of the first century, this percentage was even lower, amounting to three percent of the city's inhabitants at most. Their beliefs and way of life, as is still the case today, distinguished them clearly from the surrounding environment. And this could have two results: either derision, which could lead to intolerance, or admiration, which was expressed in various forms of sympathy, as in the case of the "God-fearing" or "proselytes," pagans who became members of the synagogue and who shared the faith in the God of Israel.

As concrete examples of this dual attitude, we can mention on the one hand the cutting opinion of an orator such as Cicero, who despised their religion and even the city of Jerusalem (cf. *Pro Flacco,* 66–69) and, on the other, the attitude of Nero's wife, Poppea, who is remembered by Flavius Josephus as a "sympathizer" of the Jews (cf. *Antichità giudaiche* 20, 195, 252; *Vita* 16), not to mention that Julius Caesar had already officially recognized specific rights of the Jews which have been recorded by the above-mentioned Jewish historian Flavius Josephus (cf. ibid., 14, 200–216). It is certain that the number of Jews, as, moreover, is still the case today, was far greater outside the land of Israel, that is, in the Diaspora, than in the territory that others called Palestine.

It is not surprising, therefore, that Paul himself was the object of the dual contradictory assessment that I mentioned. One thing is certain: the particularism of the Judaic culture and religion easily found room in an institution as far-reaching as the Roman Empire. Those who would adhere with faith to the Person of Jesus of Nazareth, Jew or Gentile, were in the more difficult and troubled position, to the extent to which they were to distinguish themselves from both Judaism and the prevalent paganism. In any case, two factors were in Paul's favor. The first was the Greek, or rather Hellenistic, culture, which, after Alexander the Great, had become a common heritage, at least of the Eastern Mediterranean and of the Middle East, and had even absorbed many elements of peoples traditionally considered barbarian. One writer of the time says in this regard that Alexander "ordered that all should consider the entire *oecumene* as their homeland . . . and that a distinction should no longer be made between Greek and barbarian" (Plutarch, *De Alexandri Magni fortuna aut virtute,* 6, 8).

The second factor was the political and administrative structure of the Roman Empire, which guaranteed peace and stability from Britain as far as southern Egypt, unifying a territory of previously unheard of dimensions. It was possible to move with sufficient freedom and safety in this space, making use, among other things, of an extraordinary network of roads and finding at every point of arrival basic cultural characteristics which, without affecting local values, nonetheless represented a common fabric of unification *super partes* (impartial), so that the Jewish philosopher, Philo of Alexandria, a contemporary of Paul himself, praised the Emperor Augustus for "composing in harmony all the savage peoples, making himself the guardian of peace" (*Legatio ad Caium,* 146–147).

There is no doubt that the universalist vision characteristic of St. Paul's personality, at least of the Christian Paul after the event on the road to Damascus, owes its basic impact to faith in Jesus Christ, since the figure of the Risen One was by this time situated beyond any particularistic narrowness. Indeed, for the Apostle "there is neither Jew nor Greek, there is neither slave nor free, there is neither male nor female; for you are all one in Christ Jesus" (Gal 3:28). Yet, even the historical and cultural situation of his time and milieu could not but have had an influence on his decisions and his work. Some have defined Paul as "a man of three cultures," taking into account his Jewish background, his Greek tongue, and his prerogative as a *civis romanus* [Roman citizen], as the name of Latin origin suggests. Particularly the Stoic philosophy dominant in Paul's time, which influenced Christianity, even if only marginally, should be recalled. Concerning this, we cannot gloss over certain names of Stoic philosophers such as those of its founders, Zeno and Cleanthes, and then those closer to Paul in time such as Seneca, Musonius, and Epictetus: in them the loftiest values of humanity and wisdom are found which were naturally to be absorbed by Christianity. As one student of the subject splendidly wrote, "Stoicism . . . announced a new ideal, which imposed upon man obligations to his peers, but at the same time set him free from all physical and national ties, and made of him a purely spiritual being" (M. Pohlenz, *La Stoa,* I, Florence, 2, 1978, p. 565f.).

One thinks, for example, of the doctrine of the universe understood as a single great harmonious body and consequently of the doctrine of equality among all people without social distinctions, of the equivalence, at least in principle, of men and women, and then of the ideal of frugality, of the just measure and self-control to avoid all excesses. When Paul wrote to the Philippians, "Whatever is true, whatever is honorable, whatever is just, whatever is pure, whatever is lovely, whatever is gracious, if there is any excellence, if there is anything worthy of praise, think about these things" (Phil 4:8), he was only taking up a purely humanistic concept proper to that philosophical wisdom.

In St. Paul's time, a crisis of traditional religion was taking place, at least in its mythological and even civil aspects. After Lucretius had already ruled polemically a century earlier that "religion has led to many misdeeds" (*De rerum natura*, 1, 101, "On the Nature of Things"), a philosopher such as Seneca, going far beyond any external ritualism, taught that "God is close to you, he is with you, he is within you" (*Epistulae morales to Lucilius*, 41, 1). Similarly, when Paul addresses an audience of Epicurean philosophers and Stoics in the Areopagus of Athens, he literally says, God "does not live in shrines made by man, . . . for 'In him we live and move and have our being'" (Acts 17:24, 28). In saying this he certainly re-echoes the Judaic faith in a God who cannot be represented in anthropomorphic terms and even places himself on a religious wavelength that his listeners knew well.

We must also take into account the fact that many pagan cults dispensed with the official temples of the town and made use of private places that favored the initiation of their followers. It is therefore not surprising that Christian gatherings (*ekklesiai*) as Paul's letters attest, also took place in private homes. At that time, moreover, there were not yet any public buildings. Therefore, Christian assemblies must have appeared to Paul's contemporaries as a simple variation of their most intimate religious practice. Yet the differences between pagan cults and Christian worship are not negligible and regard the participants' awareness of their identity as well as the participation in common of men and women, the celebration of the "Lord's Supper," and the reading of the Scriptures.

In conclusion, from this brief overview of the cultural context of the first century of the Christian era, it is clear that it is impossible to understand St. Paul properly without placing him against both the Judaic and pagan background of his time. Thus he grows in historical and spiritual stature, revealing both sharing and originality in comparison with the surrounding environment. However, this applies likewise to Christianity in general, of which the Apostle Paul, precisely, is a paradigm of the highest order from whom we all, always, still have much to learn. And this was the goal of the Pauline Year: to learn from St. Paul; to learn faith, to learn Christ, and finally to learn the way of upright living.

CHAPTER TWO

The Life of St. Paul before and after Damascus*

I would like to continue the reflection on the Apostle to the Gentiles, presenting a brief biography of him. Since we shall be dedicating the next chapter to the extraordinary event that occurred on the road to Damascus, Paul's conversion, a fundamental turning point in his life subsequent to his encounter with Christ, let us briefly pause now on his life as a whole. We find Paul's biographical details respectively in the Letter to Philemon, in which he says he is "an old man" (Philem 9: *presbytes*) and in the Acts of the Apostles, in which, at the time of the stoning of Stephen, he is described as "a young man" (7:58: *neanías*).

Both of these expressions are obviously generic, but, according to ancient calculations, a man of about 30 was described as "young" whereas he would be called "old" by the time he had reached the age of about 60. The date of Paul's birth depends largely on the dating of the Letter to Philemon. He is traditionally supposed to have written it during his imprisonment in Rome in the mid-60s. Paul would have been born in approximately the year 8. He would therefore have been about 30 at the time of the stoning of Stephen. This ought to be the correct chronology and we are celebrating the Pauline Year in accordance with precisely this chronology. The year 2008 was chosen with a date of birth of about the year 8 in mind.

In any case, Paul was born in Tarsus, Cilicia (cf. Acts 22:3). The town was the administrative capital of the region and in

---

* General Audience, August 27, 2008.

51 B.C. had had as Proconsul no less than Marcus Tullius Cicero himself, while 10 years later, in 41, Tarsus was the place where Mark Anthony and Cleopatra met for the first time. A Jew from the Diaspora, he spoke Greek although his name was of Latin origin. Moreover, it derived by assonance from the original Jewish Saul/Saulos, and he was a Roman citizen (cf. Acts 22:25–28). Paul thus appears to be at the intersection between three different cultures — Roman, Greek, and Jewish — and perhaps partly because of this was disposed for fruitful universalistic openness, for a mediation between cultures, for true universality. He also learned a manual trade, perhaps from his father, that of tentmaker (Acts 18:3: *skenopoios*). This should probably be understood as a worker of uncarded goat wool or linen fibers who made them into mats or tents (cf. Acts 20:33–35). At about the age of 12 to 13, the age in which a Jewish boy becomes a *bar mitzvah* ("son of the commandment"), Paul left Tarsus and moved to Jerusalem to be educated at the feet of Rabbi Gamaliel the Elder, a nephew of the great Rabbi Hillel, in accordance with the strictest Pharisaic norms and acquiring great zeal for the Mosaic Torah (cf. Gal 1:14; Phil 3:5–6; Acts 22:3; 23:6; 26:5).

On the basis of this profound Orthodoxy that he learned at the school of Hillel in Jerusalem, he saw the new movement that referred to Jesus of Nazareth as a risk, a threat to the Jewish identity, to the true Orthodoxy of the fathers. This explains the fact that he proudly "persecuted the Church of God" as he was to admit three times in his letters (1 Cor 15:9; Gal 1:13; Phil 3:6). Although it is not easy to imagine in what this persecution actually consisted, his attitude was intolerant. It is here that the event of Damascus fits in; we shall return to it next. It is certain that from this time Paul's life changed and he became a tireless Apostle of the Gospel. Indeed, Paul passed into history for what he did as a Christian, indeed as an Apostle, rather than as a Pharisee. Traditionally, his apostolic activity is divided on the basis of his three missionary journeys, to which can be added a fourth, his voyage to Rome as a prisoner. They are all recounted by Luke in Acts. With regard to the three missionary journeys, however, the first must be distinguished from the other two.

In fact, Paul was not directly responsible for the first (cf. Acts 13–14), which was instead entrusted to the Cypriot, Barnabas. They sailed together from Antioch on the Orontes River, sent out by that Church (cf. Acts 13:1–3) and having sailed from the port of Seleucia on the Syrian coast, crossed the island of Cyprus from Salamis to Paphos; from here they reached the southern coasts of Anatolia, today Turkey, and passed through the cities of Attalia, Perga in Pamphylia, Antioch in Pisidia, Iconium, Lystra, and Derbe, from which they returned to their starting point. Thus was born the Church of the people, the Church of the Gentiles. And in the meantime, especially in Jerusalem, a discussion had been sparked, lasting until, in order to participate truly in the promises of the prophets and enter effectively into the heritage of Israel, these Christians who came from paganism were obliged to adhere to the life and laws of Israel (various observances and prescriptions that separated Israel from the rest of the world).

To resolve this fundamental problem for the birth of the future Church, the so-called Council of the Apostles met in Jerusalem to settle on a solution, on which the effective birth of a universal Church depended. And it was decided that the observance of Mosaic Law should not be imposed upon converted pagans (cf. Acts 15:6–30): that is, they were not to be bound by the rules of Judaism; the only thing necessary was to belong to Christ, to live with Christ, and to abide by his words. Thus, in belonging to Christ, they also belonged to Abraham and to God, and were sharers in all the promises.

After this decisive event, Paul separated from Barnabas, chose Silas, and set out on his second missionary journey (Acts 15:36–18:22). Having gone beyond Syria and Cilicia, he saw once again the city of Lystra where he was joined by Timothy (a very important figure in the nascent Church, the son of a Jewish woman and a pagan), whom he had circumcised; he crossed Central Anatolia and reached the city of Troas on the northern coast of the Aegean Sea. And here another important event happened: in a dream he saw a Macedonian from the other side of the sea, that is, in Europe, who was saying, "Come and help us!" It was the Europe of the future that was asking for the light and help of the Gospel. On the impetus of this vision he set sail for Macedonia and thus entered Europe.

Having disembarked at Neapolis, he arrived at Philippi, where he founded a beautiful community. He then traveled to Thessalonica. Having left this place because of the problems the Jews created for him, he passed through Beroea to Athens. In this capital of ancient Greek culture, he preached to pagans and Greeks, first in the Agora and then on the Areopagus. And the discourse of the Areopagus, mentioned in the Acts of the Apostles, is the model of how to translate the Gospel into Greek culture, of how to make Greeks understand that this God of the Christians and Jews was not a God foreign to their culture but the unknown God they were awaiting, the true answer to the deepest questions of their culture. Then from Athens he arrived in Corinth, where he stayed for a year and a half. And here we have an event that is chronologically very reliable. It is the most reliable date in the whole of his biography because during this first stay in Corinth he was obliged to appear before the Governor of the Senatorial Province of Achaia, the Proconsul Gallio, who accused him of illegitimate worship.

In Corinth, there is an ancient inscription, found in Delphi, which mentions this Gallio and that epoch. It says that Gallio was Proconsul in Corinth between the years 51 and 53. Thus we have one absolutely certain date. Paul stayed in Corinth in those years. We may therefore suppose that he arrived there in about the year 50 and stayed until 52. Then from Corinth, passing through Cenchreae, the port on the eastern side of the city, he set sail for Palestine and arrived in Caesarea Marittima. From here he sailed for Jerusalem before returning to Antioch on the Orontes.

The third missionary journey (cf. Acts 18:23—21:16) began, like all his journeys, in Antioch, which had become the original core of the Church of the Gentiles, of the mission to the Gentiles, and was also the place where the term "Christian" was coined. It was here, St. Luke tells us, that Jesus' followers were called "Christians" for the first time. From Antioch Paul started out for Ephesus, the capital of the Province of Asia where he stayed two years, carrying out a ministry whose fruitful effects were felt throughout the region. It was from Ephesus that Paul wrote the Letters to the Thessalonians and the Corinthians. The population of the town, however, was set against him by the local silversmiths, who saw their income diminishing with the reduction in the number of those who worshipped Artemis (the temple dedicated to her in Ephesus, the *Artemysion*, was one of the seven wonders of the ancient world); Paul was thus forced to flee north. He crossed Macedonia once again and went back to Greece, probably to Corinth, where he remained for three months and wrote his famous Letter to the Romans.

From here he retraced his steps: he went back through Macedonia, reaching Troas by boat; and then, staying very briefly on the islands of Mitylene, Chios, and Samos, arrived at Miletus where he delivered an important discourse to the elders of the Church of Ephesus, outlining a portrait of a true pastor of the Church (cf. Acts 20). From here he set sail for Tyre from whence he came to Caesarea Marittima on his return journey to Jerusalem. Here he was arrested on the basis of a misunderstanding. Certain Jews had mistaken other Jews of Greek origin for Gentiles, whom Paul had taken into the temple precinct reserved for Israelites. He was spared the inevitable death sentence by the intervention of the Roman tribune on guard in the Temple area (cf. Acts 21:27–36); this happened while the imperial Procurator in Judea was Antonius Felix. After a spell in prison (the duration of which is debated), and since Paul as a Roman citizen was an appellee of Caesar (at that time Nero), the subsequent Procurator, Porcius Festus, sent him to Rome under military escort.

The voyage to Rome involved putting in at the Mediterranean islands of Crete and Malta, and then the cities of Syracuse, Rhegium Calabria, and Puteoli. The Roman Christians went down the Appian Way to meet him at the Appii Forum (about 70 km from the capital), and others went as far as Three Taverns (c. 40 km). In Rome, he met the delegates of the Jewish community, whom he told that it was for "the hope of Israel" that he was in chains (Acts 28:20). However, Luke's account ends with the mention of two years spent in Rome under mild military surveillance. Luke mentions neither a sentence of Caesar (Nero) nor, even less, the death of the accused. Later traditions speak of his liberation which would have been propitious for either a missionary journey to Spain or a subsequent episode in the East, and specifically in Crete, Ephesus, and Nicopolis in Epirus. Still, on a hypothetical basis, another arrest is conjectured and a second imprisonment in Rome (where he is supposed to have written the three so-called pastoral letters, that is, the two to Timothy and the Letter to Titus), with a second trial that would have proven unfavorable to him. Yet a series of reasons induce many scholars of St. Paul to end his biography with Luke's narrative in the Acts.

We shall return to his martyrdom later. For the time being, in this brief list of Paul's journeys, it suffices to note how dedicated he was to proclaiming the Gospel, sparing no energy, confronting a series of grave trials, of which he left us a list in the Second Letter to the Corinthians (cf. 11:21–28). Moreover, it is he who writes: "I do it all for the sake of the gospel" (1 Cor 9:23), exercising with unreserved generosity what he called "anxiety for all the churches" (2 Cor 11:28). We see a commitment that can only be explained by a soul truly fascinated by the light of the Gospel, in love with Christ, a soul sustained by profound conviction; it is necessary to bring Christ's light to the world, to proclaim the Gospel to all of us. This seems to me to be what remains for us from this brief review of St. Paul's journeys: to see his passion for the Gospel and thereby grasp the greatness, the beauty, indeed the deep need of the Gospel for all of us. Let us pray to the Lord who caused St. Paul to see his light, who made him hear his word and profoundly moved his heart, that we may also see his light, so that our hearts too may be moved by his Word and thus that we too may give the light of the Gospel and the truth of Christ to today's world which thirsts for it.

CHAPTER THREE

St. Paul's "Conversion"*

This chapter is dedicated to the experience that Paul had on his way to Damascus, and therefore on what is commonly known as his conversion. It was precisely on the road to Damascus, at the beginning of the 30s in the first century and after a period in which he had persecuted the Church that the decisive moment in Paul's life occurred. Much has been written about it and naturally from different points of view. It is certain that he reached a turning point there, indeed a reversal of perspective. And so he began, unexpectedly, to consider as "loss" and "refuse" all that had earlier constituted his greatest ideal, as it were the *raison d'être* of his life (cf. Phil 3:7–8). What had happened?

In this regard we have two types of sources. The first kind, the best known, consists of the accounts we owe to the pen of Luke, who tells of the event at least three times in the Acts of the Apostles (cf. 9:1–19; 22:3–21; 26:4–23). The average reader may be tempted to linger too long on certain details, such as the light in the sky, falling to the ground, the voice that called him, his new condition of blindness, his healing like scales falling from his eyes, and the fast that he made. But all these details refer to the heart of the event: the Risen Christ appears as a brilliant light and speaks to Saul, transforms his thinking and his entire life. The dazzling radiance of the Risen Christ blinds him; thus, what was his inner reality is also outwardly apparent, his blindness to the

---

* General Audience, September 3, 2008.

truth, to the light that is Christ. And then his definitive "yes" to Christ in Baptism restores his sight and makes him really see.

In the ancient Church, Baptism was also called "illumination," because this Sacrament gives light; it truly makes one see. In Paul, what is pointed out theologically was also brought about physically: healed of his inner blindness, he sees clearly. Thus St. Paul was not transformed by a thought but by an event, by the irresistible presence of the Risen One whom subsequently he would never be able to doubt, so powerful had been the evidence of the event, of this encounter. It radically changed Paul's life in a fundamental way; in this sense one can and must speak of a conversion. This encounter is the center of St. Luke's account for which it is very probable that he used an account that may well have originated in the community of Damascus. This is suggested by the local color, provided by Ananias's presence and by the names of both the street and the owner of the house in which Paul stayed (Acts 9:11).

The second type of source concerning the conversion consists of St. Paul's actual letters. He never spoke of this event in detail, I think because he presumed that everyone knew the essentials of his story: everyone knew that from being a persecutor he had been transformed into a fervent Apostle of Christ. And this had not happened after his own reflection, but after a powerful event, an encounter with the Risen One. Even without speaking in detail, he speaks on various occasions of this most important event, that, in other words, he too is a witness of the Resurrection of Jesus, the revelation of which he received directly from Jesus, together with his apostolic mission.

The clearest text found is in his narrative of what constitutes the center of salvation history: the death and Resurrection of Jesus and his appearances to witnesses (cf. 1 Cor 15). In the words of the ancient tradition, which he too received from the Church of Jerusalem, he says that Jesus died on the Cross, was buried, and after the Resurrection appeared risen first to Cephas, that is Peter, then to the Twelve, then to 500 brethren, most of whom were still alive at Paul's time, then to James, and then to all the Apostles. And to this account handed down by tradition he adds, "Last of all . . . he appeared also to me" (1 Cor 15:8). Thus he makes it clear that this is the foundation of his apostolate and of his new life. There are also other texts in which the same thing appears: "Jesus Christ our Lord, through whom we have received grace and apostleship" (Rom 1:4–5); and further, "Have I not seen Jesus Our Lord?" (1 Cor 9:1), words with which he alludes to something that everyone knows.

And lastly, the most widely known text is read in Galatians: "But when he who had set me apart before I was born, and had called me through his grace, was pleased to reveal his Son to me, in order that I might preach him among the Gentiles, I did not confer with flesh and blood, nor did I go up to Jerusalem to those who were Apostles before me, but I went away into Arabia; and again I returned to Damascus" (1:15–17). In this "self-apology" he definitely stresses that he is a true witness of the Risen One, that he has received his own mission directly from the Risen One.

Thus we can see that the two sources, the Acts of the Apostles and the letters of St. Paul, converge and agree on the fundamental point: the Risen One spoke to Paul, called him to the apostolate and made him a true Apostle, a witness of the Resurrection, with the specific task of proclaiming the Gospel to the Gentiles, to the Greco-Roman world. And at the same time, Paul learned that despite the immediacy of his relationship with the Risen One, he had to enter into communion with the Church, he himself had to be baptized, he had to live in harmony with the other Apostles. Only in such communion with everyone could he have been a true Apostle, as he wrote explicitly in the First Letter to the Corinthians: "Whether then it was I or they, so we preach and so you believed" (15:11). There is only one proclamation of the Risen One, because Christ is only one.

As can be seen, in all these passages Paul never once interprets this moment as an event of conversion. Why? There are many hypotheses, but for me the reason is very clear. This turning point in his life, this transformation of his whole being was not the fruit of a psychological process, of a maturation or intellectual and moral development. Rather it came from the outside: it was not the fruit of his thought but of his encounter with Jesus Christ. In this sense it was not simply a conversion, a development of his "ego," but rather a death and a resurrection for Paul himself. One existence died and another, new one was born with the Risen Christ. There is no other way in which to explain this renewal of Paul. None of the psychological analyses can clarify or solve the problem. This event alone, this powerful encounter with Christ, is the key to understanding what had happened: death and resurrection, renewal on the part of the One who had shown himself and had spoken to him. In this deeper sense we can and we must speak of conversion. This encounter is a real renewal that changed all his parameters. Now he could say that what had been essential and fundamental for him earlier had become "refuse" for him; it was no longer "gain" but loss, because henceforth the only thing that counted for him was life in Christ.

Nevertheless we must not think that Paul was thus closed in a blind event. The contrary is true because the Risen Christ is the light of truth, the light of God himself. This expanded his heart and made it open to all. At this moment he did not lose all that was good and true in his life, in his heritage, but he understood wisdom, truth, the depth of the law and of the prophets in a new way, and in a new way made them his own. At the same time, his reasoning was open to pagan wisdom. Being open to Christ with all his heart, he had become capable of an ample dialogue with everyone, he had become capable of making himself everything to everyone. Thus he could truly be the Apostle to the Gentiles.

Turning now to ourselves, let us ask what this means for us. It means that for us, too, Christianity is not a new philosophy or a new morality. We are only Christians if we encounter Christ. Of course, he does not show himself to us in this overwhelming, luminous way, as he did to Paul to make him the Apostle to all peoples. But we too can encounter Christ in reading Sacred Scripture, in prayer, in the liturgical life of the Church. We can touch Christ's Heart and feel him touching ours. Only in this personal relationship with Christ, only in this encounter with the Risen One do we truly become Christians. And in this way our reason opens, all Christ's wisdom opens as do all the riches of truth.

Therefore let us pray the Lord to illumine us, to grant us an encounter with his presence in our world, and thus to grant us a lively faith, an open heart, and great love for all, which is capable of renewing the world.

CHAPTER FOUR

St. Paul's Concept of Apostolate[*]

In the last chapter I spoke of the great turning point in St. Paul's life after his encounter with the Risen Christ. Jesus entered his life and transformed him from persecutor to Apostle. That meeting marked the start of his mission; Paul could not continue to live as he did before, he now felt that the Lord had invested him with the task of proclaiming his Gospel as an Apostle. It is precisely this new condition of life, that is, his being an Apostle of Christ, that I would like to address now. Usually, in accordance with the Gospels, it is the Twelve that we identify with the title "Apostles," thereby desiring to point out those who were Jesus' companions in life and who listened to his teaching. Yet Paul, too, felt that he was a true Apostle and it clearly appears, therefore, that the Pauline concept of "apostolate" was not limited to the group of the Twelve. Obviously, Paul is able to markedly distinguish between his own case and that of those "who were apostles before" him (Gal 1:17); he recognizes that they have a very special place in the life of the Church. Yet, as everyone knows, St. Paul understood himself as an *Apostle* in the strict sense. It is certain that at the time of the early Christians, no one covered as many miles as he did over land and across the seas, with the sole aim of proclaiming the Gospel.

Therefore, he had a concept of apostolate that went beyond the exclusive association of the term with the group of the Twelve that was passed down primarily by St. Luke in Acts (cf. Acts 1:2,

---

[*] General Audience, September 10, 2008.

26; 6:2). Indeed, in the First Letter to the Corinthians Paul makes a clear distinction between "the Twelve" and "all the apostles" mentioned as two different groups of beneficiaries of the Risen One's apparitions" (cf. 15:5, 7). In that same passage he then goes on to mention himself humbly as the "the least of the apostles," even comparing himself to "one untimely born," and declaring himself "unfit to be called an apostle, because I persecuted the Church of God. But by the grace of God I am what I am, and his grace toward me was not in vain. On the contrary, I worked harder than any of them, though it was not I, but the grace of God which is with me" (1 Cor 15:9–10).

The metaphor of the miscarriage expresses extreme humility; this will also be found in St. Ignatius of Antioch's *Epistle to the Romans*: "I am not worthy, as being the very last of them, and one born out of due time. But I have obtained mercy to be somebody, if I shall attain to God" (9, 2). What the Bishop of Antioch was to say in relation to his imminent martyrdom, foreseeing that it would reverse his condition of unworthiness, St. Paul says in relation to his own apostolic commitment: it is in this that is manifest the fruitfulness of the grace of God who knows precisely how to transform an unsuccessful man into a splendid Apostle. From a persecutor to a founder of Churches: God brought this about in one who, from the evangelical point of view, might have been considered a reject!

Therefore, according to St. Paul's conception, what is it that makes him and others Apostles? In his letters, three principal characteristics of the true Apostle appear. The first is to have "seen Jesus our Lord" (1 Cor 9:1), that is, to have had a life-changing encounter with him. Similarly, in his Letter to the Galatians (cf. 1:15–16) Paul was to say that he had been called or chosen, almost, through God's grace with the revelation of his Son, in view of proclaiming the Good News to the Gentiles. In short, it is the Lord who appoints to the apostolate and not one's own presumption. The Apostle is not made by himself but is made such by the Lord; consequently the Apostle needs to relate constantly to the Lord. Not without reason does Paul say that he is "called to be an apostle" (Rom 1:1); in other words, "an apostle — not from men nor through man, but through Jesus Christ and God the Father" (Gal 1:1). This is the first characteristic: to have seen the Lord, to have been called by him.

The second characteristic is "to have been sent." The same Greek term *apostolos* means, precisely, "sent, dispatched," that is, as ambassador and bearer of a message; he must therefore act as having been charged and as representing a sender. It is for this reason that Paul describes himself as an "apostle *of Christ Jesus*" (1 Cor 1:1; 2 Cor 1:1), that is, his delegate, placed totally at his service, even to the point that he also calls himself "a servant of Christ Jesus" (Rom 1:1). Once again the idea of someone else's initiative comes to the fore, the initiative of God in Jesus Christ, to whom Paul is fully indebted; but special emphasis is placed on the fact that Paul has received from him a mission to carry out in his name, making every personal interest absolutely secondary.

The third requisite is the task of "proclaiming the Gospel," with the consequent foundation of Churches. Indeed, the title of "Apostle" is not and cannot be honorary. It involves concretely and even dramatically the entire life of the person concerned. In his First Letter to the Corinthians, Paul exclaims: "Am I not an apostle? Have I not seen Jesus our Lord? Are not you my workmanship in the Lord?" (9:1). Similarly, in the Second Letter to the Corinthians, he says: "You yourselves are our letters of recommendation . . . a letter from Christ delivered by us, written not with ink but with the Spirit of the living God" (3:2–3).

Thus it should not come as a surprise that Chrysostom speaks of "a soul of diamond" (*Panegyrics,* 1, 8), and continues saying, "in the same way that fire, in setting light to different materials burns ever stronger. . . . So Paul's words won over to his cause all those with whom he came into contact, and those who were hostile to him, captivated by his discourses, became the fuel of this spiritual fire" (ibid., 7, 11). This explains why Paul defines the Apostles as "fellow workers" of God (1 Cor 3:9; 2 Cor 6:1), whose grace acts within them. A typical element of a true Apostle, which St. Paul highlights effectively, is a sort of identification between Gospel and evangelizer, both destined to the same fate. In fact no one emphasized as well as Paul that the proclamation of the Cross of Christ appears "a stumbling block . . . and folly" (1 Cor 1:23), to which many react with incomprehension and rejection. This happened then and it should not come as a surprise that it also happens today.

Consequently, the Apostle shares in this destiny, in appearing as "a stumbling block . . . and folly," and Paul is aware of it; this is the experience of his life. He writes to the Corinthians, not without a vein of irony: "For I think that God has exhibited us apostles as last of all, like men sentenced to death; because we have become a spectacle to the world, to angels and to men. We are fools for Christ's sake, but you are wise in Christ. We are weak, but you are strong. You are held in honor, but we in disrepute. To the present hour we hunger and thirst, we are poorly clothed and buffeted and homeless, and we labor, working with our own hands. When reviled, we bless; when persecuted, we endure; when slandered, we try to conciliate; we have become, and are now, as the refuse of the world, the dregs of all things" (1 Cor 4:9–13). This is a self-portrait of St. Paul's apostolic life: in all this suffering, the joy of being a herald of God's blessing and of the grace of the Gospel prevails.

Paul, moreover, shares with the Stoic philosophy of his time the idea of a tenacious constancy in all the difficulties that arise; but he overcomes the merely humanistic perspective by recalling the element of the love of God and of Christ: "Who shall separate us from the love of Christ? Shall tribulation, or distress, or persecution, or famine, or nakedness, or peril, or sword? As it is written, 'For your sake we are being killed all the day long; we are regarded as sheep to be slaughtered.' No, in all these things we are more than conquerors through him who loved us. For I am sure that neither death, nor life, nor angels, nor principalities, nor things present, nor things to come, nor powers, nor height, nor depth, nor anything else in all creation, will be able to separate us from the love of God in Christ Jesus our Lord" (Rom 8:35–39). This is the certainty, the profound joy that guides the Apostle Paul through all these vicissitudes: nothing can separate us from the love of God and this love is the true treasure of human life.

As can be seen, St. Paul gave himself to the Gospel with his entire existence; we could say 24 hours a day! And he exercised his ministry with faithfulness and joy, "that I might by all means save some" (1 Cor 9:22). And with regard to the Church, even knowing that he had a relationship of fatherhood with her (cf. 1 Cor 4:15), if not actually of motherhood (cf. Gal 4:19), he adopted an attitude of complete service, declaring admirably: "Not that we lord it over your faith; we work with you for your joy" (2 Cor 1:24). This remains the mission of all Christ's Apostles in all times: to be his fellow workers in true joy.

CHAPTER FIVE

Paul, the Twelve, and the Pre-Pauline Church*

I would like to address the relationship between St. Paul and the Apostles who had preceded him in following Jesus. These relations were always marked by profound respect and that frankness in Paul that stemmed from defending the truth of the Gospel. Although he was virtually a contemporary of Jesus of Nazareth, he never had the opportunity to meet him during his public life. For this reason, after being blinded on the road to Damascus, he felt the need to consult the Teacher's first disciples, those whom he had chosen to take the Gospel to the ends of the earth.

In his Letter to the Galatians, Paul wrote an important account of the contacts he had had with some of the Twelve: first of all with Peter who had been chosen as *Kephas,* the Aramaic term which means rock, on whom the Church was being built (cf. Gal 1:18), with James, "the Lord's brother" (cf. Gal 1:19), and with John (cf. Gal 2:9). Paul does not hesitate to recognize them as "pillars" of the Church. Particularly important is his meeting with Cephas (Peter), in Jerusalem: Paul stayed with him for 15 days in order to "consult him" (cf. Gal 1:18), that is, to learn about the earthly life of the Risen One who had "taken hold" of him on the road to Damascus and was radically transforming his life; from a persecutor of God's Church he had become an evangelizer of that faith in the Crucified Messiah and Son of God which in the past he had sought to destroy (cf. Gal 1:23).

---

* General Audience, September 24, 2008.

What sort of information did Paul gather about Jesus Christ during the three years that succeeded the Damascus encounter? In the First Letter to the Corinthians, we may note two passages that Paul learned in Jerusalem and that were already formulated as central elements of the Christian tradition, a constitutive tradition. Paul passed them on verbally, as he had received them, with a very solemn formula: "For I delivered to you as of first importance what I also received." He insists, therefore, on the fidelity to what he himself has received and faithfully transmits to new Christians. These are constitutive elements and concern the Eucharist and the Resurrection; they are passages that were already formulated in the 30s. Thus we come to Jesus' death, his burial in the heart of the earth, and his Resurrection (cf. 1 Cor 15:3–4).

Let us take both passages. For Paul, Jesus' words at the Last Supper (cf. 1 Cor 11:23–25) are truly the center of the Church's life: the Church is built on this center, thus becoming herself. In addition to this Eucharistic center, in which the Church is constantly reborn — also in all of St. Paul's theology, in all of his thought — these words have a considerable impact on Paul's personal relationship with Jesus. On the one hand they testify that the Eucharist illumines the curse of the Cross, making it a blessing (Gal 3:13–14), and on the other, they explain the importance of Jesus' death and Resurrection. In St. Paul's letters, the "for you" of the Institution of the Eucharist is personalized, becoming "for me" (Gal 2:20) — since Paul realized that in that "you" he himself was known and loved by Jesus — as well as being "for all" (2 Cor 5:14). This "for you" becomes "for me" and "for her [the Church]" (Eph 5:25), that is, "for all," in the expiatory sacrifice of the Cross (cf. Rom 3:25). The Church is built from — and in — the Eucharist and recognizes that she is the "Body of Christ" (1 Cor 12:27), nourished every day by the power of the Spirit of the Risen One.

The other text, on the Resurrection, once again passes on to us the same formula of fidelity. St. Paul writes: "For I delivered to you as of first importance what I also received, that Christ died for our sins in accordance with the Scriptures, that he was buried, that he was raised on the third day in accordance with the Scriptures, and that he appeared to Cephas, then to the Twelve" (1 Cor 15:3–5). This "for our sins" also recurs in this tradition passed on to Paul, which places the emphasis on the gift that Jesus made of himself to the Father in order to set us free from sin and death. From this gift of Jesus himself, Paul draws the most engaging and fascinating expressions of our relationship with Christ: "For our sake he made him to be sin who knew no sin, so that in him we might become the righteousness of God" (2 Cor 5:21); "You know the grace of our Lord Jesus Christ, that though he was rich, yet for your sake he became poor, so that by his poverty you might become rich" (2 Cor 8:9). Worth remembering is the comment Martin Luther made, then an Augustinian monk, on these paradoxical words of Paul: "This is that mystery which is rich in divine grace to sinners, wherein by a wonderful exchange our sins are no longer ours but Christ's, and the righteousness of Christ is not Christ's but ours" (*Comments on the Psalms* of 1513–1515). And thus we are saved.

In the original *kerygma* (announcement), passed on by word of mouth, the use of the verb "is risen" rather than "was risen" — which would have been more logical to use, in continuity with "died . . . and was buried" — deserves mention. The verb form "is risen" has been chosen to stress that Christ's Resurrection has an effect on the existence of believers even today; we might translate it as: "is risen and continues to live" in the Eucharist and in the Church. Thus all the Scriptures bear witness to the death and Resurrection of Christ because, as Ugo di San Vittore was to write, "the whole of divine Scripture constitutes one book and this one book is Christ, for the whole of Scripture speaks of Christ and is fulfilled in Christ" (*De arca Noe,* 2, 8). If St. Ambrose of Milan could say that "in Scripture we read Christ," it is because the early Church reinterpreted all the Scriptures of Israel, starting from and returning to Christ.

The enumeration of the apparitions of the Risen One to Cephas, to the Twelve, to more than 500 brethren, and to James, culminates with the mention of the apparition to Paul himself on the road to Damascus: "Last of all, as to one untimely born" (1 Cor 15:8). Since he had persecuted God's Church, in this confession he expresses his unworthiness to be considered an Apostle on a par with those who had preceded him, but God's grace within him was not in vain (1 Cor 15:10). Thus, the overwhelming affirmation of divine grace unites Paul with the first witnesses of Christ's Resurrection: "Whether then it was I or they, so we preach and so you believed" (1 Cor 15:11). The identity and unity of the Gospel proclamation is important; both they and I preach the same faith, the same Gospel of Jesus Christ who died and is risen and who gives himself in the Most Holy Eucharist.

The importance that he confers on the living Tradition of the Church, which she passes on to her communities, shows how mistaken is the view that attributes the invention of Christianity to Paul; before evangelizing on behalf of Jesus Christ, his Lord, Paul has met him on the road to Damascus and visited him in the Church, observing his life in the Twelve and in those who followed him on the roads of Galilee. In the next Catecheses, we will have the opportunity to examine the contributions that Paul made to the Church of the origins. However, the mission he received from the Risen One to evangelize the Gentiles needed to be confirmed and guaranteed by those who offered him and Barnabas their right hand in fellowship, as a sign of approval of their apostolate and their evangelization and of their acceptance into the one communion of Christ's Church (cf. Gal 2:9). One then understands that the expression "even though we once regarded Christ according to the flesh" (2 Cor 5:16) does not mean that his earthly life has little importance for our development in the faith, but that since his Resurrection our way of relating to him has changed. He is at the same time the Son of God "who was descended from David according to the flesh and designated Son of God in power according to the Spirit of holiness by his Resurrection from the dead," as Paul was to recall at the beginning of his Letter to the Romans (1:3–4).

The more we try to trace the footsteps of Jesus of Nazareth on the roads of Galilee, the better we shall be able to understand that he took on our humanity, sharing it in all things except sin. Our faith is not born from a myth or from an idea, but from the encounter with the Risen One in the life of the Church.

CHAPTER SIX

The "Council" of Jerusalem and the Incident in Antioch[*]

Paul's relationship with the Twelve was always one of respect and veneration that did not fail when he defended the truth of the Gospel, which is nothing if not Jesus Christ, the Lord. Let us reflect today on two episodes that show the veneration and at the same time the freedom with which the Apostle addresses Cephas and the other Apostles: the so-called "Council" of Jerusalem and the incident in Antioch, Syria, mentioned in the Letter to the Galatians (cf. 2:1–10; 2:11–14).

In the Church, every Council and Synod is an "event of the Spirit" which considers the petitions of all the People of God as it takes place. This was experienced first-hand by all those who received the gift of participating in the Second Vatican Council. For this reason, St. Luke, in telling us about the Church's First Council, held in Jerusalem, introduces the letter which the Apostles sent on that occasion to the Christian communities in the Diaspora: "It has seemed good to the Holy Spirit and to us" (Acts 15:28). The Spirit, who works in the whole Church, takes the Apostles by the hand, leading them on new roads to implement his plans; he is the principal artisan who builds the Church.

And the Assembly of Jerusalem also took place at a time of no small tension in the primitive community. It was a matter of settling the question of whether or not circumcision was compulsory for the Gentiles who were adhering to Jesus Christ, the

* General Audience, October 1, 2008.

Lord, or whether it was lawful for them not to be bound by the Mosaic law, that is, the observance of the norms required in order to be upright, law-abiding people, and especially, not to be bound by those norms that concerned religious purification, clean and unclean foods, and the Sabbath. Paul also refers to the Assembly of Jerusalem in Gal 2:1–10; 14 years after his encounter with the Risen One at Damascus — we are in the second half of the 40s — Paul set out with Barnabas from Antioch in Syria, taking with him Titus, his faithful collaborator who, although he was a Greek, had not been obliged to be circumcised in order to join the Church. On that occasion Paul explained to the Twelve, whom he describes as those who were "of repute," his Gospel of freedom from the Law (cf. Gal 2:6). In the light of the encounter with the Risen Christ, Paul realized that as soon as they adhered to the Gospel of Jesus Christ, the Gentiles no longer needed as a hallmark of justice either circumcision or the rules that governed food and the Sabbath: Christ is our justice and all things that conform to him are "just." No other signs are necessary in order to be just.

In the Letter to the Galatians, St. Paul tells in a few lines how the assembly went. He says enthusiastically that the Gospel of freedom from the Law was approved by James, Cephas, and John, "the pillars," who offered him and Barnabas the right hand of ecclesial communion in Christ (cf. Gal 2:9). Since, as we have noted, for Luke the Council of Jerusalem expresses the action of the Holy Spirit, for Paul it represents the crucial recognition of freedom shared among all who participate in it: a freedom from the obligations that derive from circumcision and from the Law; that freedom for which "Christ has set us free" so that we might stand fast and not submit again to a yoke of slavery (cf. Gal 5:1). The two accounts of Paul and Luke of the Assembly of Jerusalem have in common the liberating action of the Spirit, for "where the Spirit of the Lord is, there is freedom," Paul was to say in his Second Letter to the Corinthians (cf. 3:17).

However, as very clearly appears in St. Paul's letters, Christian freedom is never identified with libertinage or with the will to do as one pleases; it is actuated in conformity to Christ and hence in authentic service to the brethren and above all to the neediest. For this reason Paul's account of the Assembly ends by recalling the Apostles' recommendation to him: "Only they would have us remember the poor, which very thing I was eager to do" (Gal 2:10). Every Council is born from the Church and returns to the Church: in this case it returns with an attention for the poor who are primarily of the Church of Jerusalem, as seen in various annotations in Paul's letters. In his concern for the poor, to which he testifies in particular in his Second Letter to the Corinthians (cf. 8–9), and in the final part of his Letter to the Romans (cf. Rom 15), Paul demonstrates his fidelity to the decisions made at the Assembly.

Perhaps we are no longer able to understand fully the meaning that Paul and his communities attributed to the collection for the poor of Jerusalem. It was a completely new initiative in the area of religious activities: it was not obligatory, but free and spontaneous; all the Churches that were founded by Paul in the West took part. The collection expressed the community's debt to the Mother Church of Palestine, from which they had received the ineffable gift of the Gospel. The value that Paul attributes to this gesture of sharing is so great that he seldom calls it merely a "collection." Rather, for him it is "service," "blessing," "gift," "grace," even "liturgy" (cf. 2 Cor 9).

Particularly surprising is the latter term which gives a value that is even religious to a collection of money: on the one hand it is a liturgical act or "service" offered by every community to God; and on the other, it is a loving action made for people.

Love for the poor and the divine liturgy go hand in hand; love for the poor is liturgy. The two horizons are present in every liturgy that is celebrated and experienced in the Church which, by her nature, is opposed to any separation between worship and life, between faith and works, between prayer and charity for the brethren. Thus, the Council of Jerusalem came into being to settle the question of how to treat Gentiles who came to the faith, opting for freedom from circumcision and from the observances imposed by the Law, and it was settled by the ecclesial and pastoral need that is centered on faith in Jesus Christ and love for the poor of Jerusalem and the whole Church.

The second episode is the well-known incident in Antioch, Syria, that attests to the inner freedom Paul enjoyed: How should one behave when eating with believers of both Jewish and Gentile origin? Here the other epicenter of Mosaic observance emerges: the distinction between clean and unclean foods which deeply separated practicing Jews from Gentiles. At the outset, Cephas, Peter, shared meals with both; but with the arrival of certain Christians associated with James, "the Lord's brother" (Gal 1:19), Peter began to avoid contact with Gentiles at the table in order not to shock those who were continuing to observe the laws governing the cleanliness of food, and his decision was shared by Barnabas. This decision profoundly divided the Christians who had come from circumcision and the Christians who came from paganism. This behavior, that was a real threat to the unity and freedom of the Church, provoked a passionate reaction in Paul who even accused Peter and the others of hypocrisy: "If you, though a Jew, live like a Gentile and not like a Jew, how can you compel the Gentiles to live like Jews?" (Gal 2:14).

In fact, the thoughts of Paul on the one hand, and of Peter and Barnabas on the other, were different: for the latter the separation from the Gentiles was a way to safeguard and not to shock believers who came from Judaism; on the contrary, for Paul it constituted the danger of a misunderstanding of the universal salvation in Christ, offered both to Gentiles and Jews. If justification is only achieved by virtue of faith in Christ, of conformity with him, regardless of any effect of the Law, what is the point of continuing to observe the cleanliness of foods at shared meals? In all likelihood the approaches of Peter and Paul were different: the former did not want to lose the Jews who had adhered to the Gospel, and the latter did not want to diminish the saving value of Christ's death for all believers.

It is strange to say but in writing to the Christians of Rome a few years later (in about the middle of the 50s), Paul was to find himself facing a similar situation and asked the strong not to eat unclean foods in order not to lose or scandalize the weak: "It is right not to eat meat or drink wine or do anything that makes your brother stumble" (Rom 14:21). The incident at Antioch thus proved to be as much of a lesson for Peter as it was for Paul. Only sincere dialogue, open to the truth of the Gospel, could guide the Church on her journey: "For the kingdom of God does not mean food and drink but righteousness and peace and joy in the Holy Spirit" (Rom 14:17). It is a lesson that we too must learn: with the different *charisms* entrusted to Peter and to Paul, let us all allow ourselves to be guided by the Spirit, seeking to live in the freedom that is guided by faith in Christ and expressed in service to the brethren. It is essential to be conformed ever more closely to Christ. In this way one becomes really free, in this way the Law's deepest core is expressed within us: love for God and neighbor. Let us pray the Lord that he will teach us to share his sentiments, to learn from him true freedom and the evangelical love that embraces every human being.

CHAPTER SEVEN

The Relationship with
the Historical Jesus[*]

In the last chapter, I spoke of Paul's encounter with the Risen Christ that profoundly changed his life and then of his relationship with the Twelve Apostles called by Jesus — especially his relationship with James, Cephas, and John — and of his relationship with the Church in Jerusalem.

The question remains as to what St. Paul knew about the earthly Jesus, about his life, his teachings, his Passion. Before entering into this topic, it might be useful to bear in mind that St. Paul himself distinguishes between two ways of knowing Jesus, and more generally, two ways of knowing a person. He writes in his Second Letter to the Corinthians: "From now on, therefore, we regard no one according to the flesh; even though we once regarded Christ according to the flesh, we regard him thus no longer" (5:16). Knowing "according to the flesh," or from a human point of view, means knowing solely in an external way, by means of external criteria: one may have seen a person various times and hence be familiar with his features and various characteristics of his behavior: how he speaks, how he moves, etc. Although one may know someone in this way, nevertheless one does not really know him, one does not know the essence of the person. Only with the heart does one truly know a person.

Indeed, the Pharisees and the Sadducees were externally acquainted with Jesus, they learned his teaching and knew many

---

[*] General Audience, October 8, 2008.

details about him but they did not know him in his truth. There is a similar distinction in one of Jesus' sayings. After the Transfiguration he asked the Apostles: "Who do men say that the Son of man is?" and "Who do you say that I am?" The people know him, but superficially; they know various things about him, but they do not really know him. On the other hand, the Twelve, thanks to the friendship that calls the heart into question, have at least understood in substance and begun to discover who Jesus is. This different manner of knowing still exists today: there are learned people who know many details about Jesus and simple people who have no knowledge of these details but have known him in his truth, "Heart speaks to heart." And Paul wants to say that to know Jesus essentially in this way, with the heart, is to know the person essentially in his truth; and then, a little later, to get to know him better.

Having said this, the question still remains: What did St. Paul know about Jesus' practical life, his words, his Passion, and his miracles? It seems certain that he did not meet him during his earthly life. Through the Apostles and the nascent Church Paul certainly must have come to know the details of Jesus' earthly life. In his letters, we may find three forms of reference to the pre-Paschal Jesus. In the first place, there are explicit and direct references. Paul speaks of Jesus' Davidic genealogy (cf. Rom 1:3), he knows of the existence of his "brethren" or kin (1 Cor 9:5; Gal 1:19), he knows the sequence of events of the Last Supper (cf. 1 Cor 11:23), and he knows other things that Jesus said, for example on the indissolubility of marriage (cf. 1 Cor 7:10 with Mk 10:11–12) and on the need for those who proclaim the Gospel to be supported by the community since the laborer deserves his wages (cf. 1 Cor 9:14, with Lk 10:7). Paul knows the words that Jesus spoke at the Last Supper (cf. 1 Cor 11:24–25, with Lk 22:19–20), and also knows Jesus' Cross. These are direct references to words and events of Jesus' life.

In the second place, we can glimpse in a few sentences of the Pauline letters various allusions to the tradition attested to in the Synoptic Gospels. For example, the words we read in the First Letter to the Thessalonians which say that "the day of the Lord will come like a thief in the night" (5:2), could not be explained with a reference to the Old Testament prophesies, since the comparison with the nocturnal thief is only found in the Gospels of Matthew and of Luke, hence it is indeed taken from the Synoptic tradition. Thus, when we read: "God chose what is foolish in the world" (1 Cor 1:27–28), one hears the faithful echo of Jesus' teaching on the simple and the poor (cf. Mt 5:3; 11:25; 19:30). Then there are the words that Jesus spoke at the messianic jubilee: "I thank you, Father, Lord of heaven and earth, that you have hidden these things from the wise and understanding and revealed them to infants" (Mt 11:25). Paul knows — from his missionary experience — how true these words are; that is, that the hearts of the simple are open to knowledge of Jesus.

Even the reference to Jesus' obedience "unto death," which we read in Philippians 2:8, can only recall the earthly Jesus' unreserved readiness to do his Father's will (cf. Mk 3:35; Jn 4:34). Paul is thus acquainted with Jesus' Passion, his Cross, the way in which he lived the last moments of his life. The Cross of Jesus and the tradition concerning this event of the Cross lie at the heart of the Pauline *kerygma* (proclamation). Another pillar of Jesus' life known to St. Paul is the "Sermon on the Mount," from which he cited certain elements almost literally when writing to the Romans: "Love one another. . . . Bless those who persecute you. . . . Live in harmony with one another . . . overcome evil with good. . . ." Therefore, in his letters the Sermon on the Mount is faithfully reflected (cf. Mt 5–7).

Lastly, it is possible to individuate a third manner in which Jesus' words are present in St. Paul's letters: it is when he brings about a form of transposition of the pre-Paschal tradition to the situation after Easter. A typical case is the theme of the Kingdom of God. It was certainly at the heart of the historical Jesus' preaching (cf. Mt 3:2; Mk 1:15; Lk 4:43). It is possible to note in Paul a transposition of this subject because, after the Resurrection, it is obvious that Jesus in person, the Risen One, is the Kingdom of God. The Kingdom therefore arrives where Jesus is arriving. Thus the theme of the Kingdom of God, in which Jesus' mystery was anticipated, is transformed into Christology.

Yet, the same attitudes that Jesus requested for entering the Kingdom of God apply precisely to Paul with regard to justification through faith: both entry into the Kingdom and justification demand an approach of deep humility and openness, free from presumptions, in order to accept God's grace. For example, the parable of the Pharisee and the publican (cf. Lk 18:9–14) imparts a teaching that is found exactly as it is in Paul, when he insists on the proper exclusion of any boasting to God. Even Jesus' sentences on publicans and prostitutes, who were more willing to accept the Gospel than the Pharisees (cf. Mt 21:31; Lk 7:36–50), and his decision to share meals with them (cf. Mt 9:10–13; Lk 15:1–2) are fully confirmed in Paul's teaching on God's merciful love for sinners (cf. Rom 5:8–10; Eph 2:3–5). Thus the theme of the Kingdom of God is reproposed in a new form, but always in full fidelity to the tradition of the historical Jesus.

Another example of the faithful transformation of the doctrinal nucleus imparted by Jesus is found in the "titles" he uses. Before Easter he described himself as the Son of man; after Easter it becomes obvious that the Son of man is also the Son of God. Therefore, Paul's favorite title to describe Jesus is *Kýrios,* "Lord" (cf. Phil 2:9–11), which suggests Jesus' divinity. The Lord Jesus, with this title, appears in the full light of the Resurrection. On the Mount of Olives, at the moment of Jesus' extreme anguish, (cf. Mk 14:36), the disciples, before falling asleep, had heard him talking to the Father and calling him *"Abba,* Father." This is a very familiar word equivalent to our "Daddy," used only by children in talking to their father. Until that time it had been unthinkable for a Jew to use such a word in order to address God; but Jesus, being a true Son, at that moment of intimacy used this form and said: "Abba, Father." Surprisingly, in St. Paul's Letters to the Romans and to the Galatians, this word "Abba," that expresses the exclusivity of Jesus' sonship, appears on the lips of the baptized (cf. Rom 8:15; Gal 4:6) because they have received the "Spirit of the Son." They now carry this Spirit within them and can speak like Jesus and with Jesus as true children to their Father; they can say "Abba" because they have become sons in the Son.

And finally, I would like to mention the saving dimension of Jesus' death that we find in the Gospel saying, according to which, "the Son of Man also came not to be served but to serve, and to give his life as a ransom for many" (Mk 10:45; Mt 20:28). A faithful reflection of these words of Jesus appears in the Pauline teaching on the death of Jesus as having been bought at a price (cf. 1 Cor 6:20), as redemption (cf. Rom 3:24), as liberation (cf. Gal 5:1), and as reconciliation (cf. Rom 5:10; 2 Cor 5:18–20). This is the center of Pauline theology that is founded on these words of Jesus.

To conclude, St. Paul did not think of Jesus in historical terms, as a person of the past. He certainly knew the great tradition of the life, words, death, and Resurrection of Jesus, but does not treat all this as something from the past; he presents it as the reality of the living Jesus. For Paul, Jesus' words and actions do not belong to the historical period, to the past. Jesus is alive now, he speaks to us now and lives for us. This is the true way to know Jesus and to understand the tradition about him. We must also learn to know Jesus not from the human point of view, as a person of the past, but as our Lord and Brother, who is with us today and shows us how to live and how to die.

CHAPTER EIGHT

Paul's Ecclesiological Dimension*

In the last chapter I spoke of Paul's relationship with the pre-Paschal Jesus in his earthly life. The question was: "What did Paul know about Jesus' life, his words, his Passion?" Today I would like to speak about St. Paul's teaching on the Church. We must start by noting that this word *"Chiesa"* in Italian, as in French *"Église,"* and in Spanish *"Iglesia,"* comes from the Greek *"ekklesia."* It comes from the Old Testament and means "the assembly of the People of Israel, convoked by God." It particularly means the exemplary assembly at the foot of Mount Sinai. This word now means the new community of believers in Christ who feel that they are God's assembly, the new convocation of all the peoples by God and before him. The term *ekklesia* comes for the first time from the pen of Paul, the first author of a Christian text. It makes its first appearance in the *incipit* of his First Letter to the Thessalonians, where Paul textually addresses "the Church of the Thessalonians" (cf. also "the Church of the Laodiceans" in Col 4:16). In other letters he speaks of the Church of God which is at Corinth (1 Cor 1:2; 2 Cor 1:1) and of the Churches of Galatia (Gal 1:2, etc.), particular Churches therefore, but he also says he persecuted *"the* Church of God": not a specific local community, but "the Church of God." Thus we see that this word, "Church," has a multi-dimensional meaning: it indicates a part of God's assembly in a specific place (a city, a country, a house) but it also means the Church as a whole. And thus we see that "the Church

---

* General Audience, October 15, 2008.

of God" is not only a collection of various local Churches but that these various local Churches in turn make up one Church of God. All together they are "the Church of God" which precedes the individual local Churches and is expressed or brought into being in them.

It is important to observe that the word "Church" almost always appears with the additional qualification "of God": she is not a human association, born from ideas or common interests, but a convocation of God. He has convoked her, thus, in all her manifestations she is one. The oneness of God creates the oneness of the Church in all the places in which she is found. Later, in the Letter to the Ephesians, Paul richly elaborated the concept of the Church's oneness, in continuity with the concept of the People of God, Israel, considered by the prophets as "God's bride" called to live in a spousal relationship with him. Paul presents the one Church of God as "Christ's bride" in love, one body and one spirit with Christ himself. It is well known that as a young man Paul was a fierce adversary of the new movement constituted by the Church of Christ. He was opposed to this new movement because he saw it as a threat to fidelity to the tradition of the People of God, inspired by faith in the one God. This fidelity was expressed above all in circumcision, in the observance of the rules of religious purity, abstention from certain foods, and respect for the Sabbath. The Israelites had paid for this fidelity with the blood of martyrs in the period of the Maccabees, when the Hellenistic regime wanted to force all peoples to conform to the one Hellenistic culture. Many Israelites spilled their blood to defend the proper vocation of Israel. The martyrs paid with their lives for the identity of their people who expressed themselves through these elements. After his encounter with the Risen Christ, Paul understood that Christians were not traitors; on the contrary, in the new situation the God of Israel, through Christ, had extended his call to all the peoples, becoming the God of all peoples. In this way fidelity to the one God was achieved. Distinctive signs constituted by special rules and observances were no longer necessary since all were called, in their variety, to belong to the one People of God in the "Church of God" in Christ.

One thing was immediately clear to Paul in his new situation: the fundamental, foundational value of Christ and of the "word" that he was proclaiming. Paul knew not only that one does not become Christian by coercion but also that in the internal configuration of the new community the institutional element was inevitably linked to the living "word," to the proclamation of the living Christ through whom God opens himself to all peoples and unites them in one People of God. It is symptomatic that in the Acts of the Apostles Luke twice uses, also with regard to Paul, the phrase "to speak the word" (cf. Acts 4:29, 31; 8:25; 11:19; 13:46; 14:25; 16:6, 32) evidently with the intention of giving the maximum emphasis to the crucial importance of the "word" of proclamation. In practice this word is constituted by the Cross and the Resurrection of Christ in which the Scriptures found fulfillment. The Paschal Mystery, which brought the Apostle to the turning point in his life on the road to Damascus, obviously lies at the heart of his preaching (1 Cor 2:2; 15:14). This Mystery, proclaimed in the Word, is brought about in the Sacraments of Baptism and of the Eucharist and then becomes reality in Christian love. Paul's only goal in his work of evangelization is to establish the community of believers in Christ. This idea is inherent in the actual etymology of the term *ekklesia,* which Paul, and with him all Christendom, preferred to the term "synagogue": not only because the former is originally more "secular" (deriving from the Greek practice of the political assembly which was not exactly religious), but also because it directly involves the more theological idea of a call *ab extra* (from outside), and is not, therefore, a mere gathering; believers are called by God, who gathers them in a community, his Church.

Along these lines we can also understand the original concept of the Church exclusively Pauline as the "Body of Christ." In this regard it is necessary to bear in mind the two dimensions of this concept. One is sociological in character, according to which the body is made up of its elements and would not exist without them. This interpretation appears in the Letter to the Romans and in the First Letter to the Corinthians, in which Paul uses an image that already existed in Roman sociology: he says that a people is like a body with its different parts, each of which has its own function but all together, even its smallest and seemingly most insignificant parts are necessary if this body is to be able to live and carry out its functions. The Apostle appropriately observes that in the Church there are many vocations: prophets, apostles, teachers, simple people, all are called to practice charity every day, all are necessary in order to build the living unity of this spiritual organism. The other interpretation refers to the actual Body of Christ. Paul holds that the Church is not only an organism but really becomes the Body of Christ in the Sacrament of the Eucharist, where we all receive his Body and really become his Body. Thus is brought about the spousal mystery that all become one body and one spirit in Christ. So it is that the reality goes far beyond any sociological image, expressing its real, profound essence, that is, the oneness of all the baptized in Christ, considered by the Apostle "one" in Christ, conformed to the Sacrament of his Body.

In saying this, Paul shows that he knows well and makes us all understand that the Church is not his and is not ours: the Church is the Body of Christ, it is a Church *of God*, "God's field, God's building . . . God's temple" (1 Cor 3:9, 16). This latter designation is particularly interesting because it attributes to a fabric of interpersonal relations a term that commonly served to mean a physical place, considered sacred. The relationship between church and temple therefore comes to assume two complementary dimensions: on the one hand the characteristic of separateness and purity that the sacred building deserved is applied to the ecclesial community, but on the other, the concept of a material space is also overcome, to transfer this quality to the reality of a living community of faith. If previously temples had been considered places of God's presence, it was now known and seen that God does not dwell in buildings made of stone but that the place of God's presence in the world is the living community of believers.

The description "People of God" would deserve a separate commentary. In Paul, it is applied mainly to the People of the Old Testament and then to the Gentiles, who were "the non-people" but also became People of God thanks to their insertion in Christ through the word and sacrament.

And finally, one last nuance. In his Letter to Timothy, Paul describes the Church as the "household of God" (1 Tim 3:15); and this is a truly original definition because it refers to the Church as a community structure in which warm, family-type interpersonal relations are lived. The Apostle helps us to understand ever more deeply the mystery of the Church in her different dimensions as an assembly of God in the world. This is the greatness of the Church and the greatness of our call; we are a temple of God in the world, a place in which God truly dwells, and at the same time we are a community, a family of God who is love. As a family and home of God, we must practice God's love in the world and thus, with the power that comes from faith, be a place and a sign of his presence. Let us pray the Lord to grant us to be increasingly his Church, his Body, the place where his love is present in this world of ours and in our history.

CHAPTER NINE

The Importance of Christology: Pre-Existence and Incarnation*

In previous chapters we have meditated on St. Paul's "conversion," the result of his personal encounter with the Crucified and Risen Jesus, and we asked ourselves what relationship the Apostle to the Gentiles had with the earthly Jesus. Today I would like to speak of the teaching that St. Paul bequeathed to us on the *centrality of the Risen Christ in the mystery of salvation,* on his Christology. In truth, the Risen Jesus Christ, "exalted above every other name," is at the center of every reflection Paul makes. Christ, for the Apostle, is the criterion for evaluating events and things, the goal of every effort that he makes to proclaim the Gospel, the great passion that sustains his footsteps on the roads of the world. And this is a real and living Christ: "Christ," Paul says, ". . . who loved me and gave himself for me" (Gal 2:20). This person who loves me, with whom I can speak, who listens to me and answers me, this is truly the starting point for understanding the world and finding the way through history.

Those who have read St. Paul's writings know well that he was not concerned to recount the sequence of individual events in Jesus' life. Nevertheless we may think that in his catechesis he told far more about the pre-Paschal Jesus than he writes in his letters which are admonitions in precise situations. His pastoral

---

* General Audience, October 22, 2008.

and theological intention was so focused on fostering the nascent communities that it came naturally to him to concentrate completely on the proclamation of Jesus Christ as "Lord," alive now and present now among his followers. Hence the characteristic essentiality of Pauline Christology, which develops the depths of the mystery with a constant and precise concern: to proclaim the living Jesus, of course, but above all to proclaim the central reality of his death and Resurrection as the culmination of his earthly existence and the root of the successive development of the whole Christian faith, the whole reality of the Church.

For the Apostle the Resurrection is not an event in itself, separate from death: the Risen One is always the One who has first been crucified. Even as the Risen One he bears his wounds: the Passion is present in him and we can say, together with Pascal (the great French thinker Blaise Pascal, 1623–1662), that he is the Suffering One until the end of the world, while at the same time being the Risen One and living with us and for us. Paul had understood this identification of the Risen One with the Crucified Christ at the encounter on the road to Damascus: at that moment it was clearly revealed to him that the Crucified One is the Risen One and the Risen One is the Crucified One, who asks Paul, "Why do you persecute me?" (Acts 9:4). Paul is persecuting Christ in the Church and then realizes that the Cross is not "accursed by God" (Deut 21:23), but is also the sacrifice for our redemption.

Fascinated, the Apostle contemplates the hidden secret of the Crucified and Risen One and, through the suffering experienced by Christ in his humanity (*earthly dimension*), goes back to that eternal existence in which he is wholly one with the Father (*dimension before time*): "When the time had fully come," he wrote, "God sent forth his son, born of woman, born under the law, to redeem those who were under the law, so that we might receive adoption as sons" (Gal 4:4–5). These two dimensions, his eternal *pre-existence* with the Father and the Lord's descent in his *Incarnation* are already announced in the Old Testament, in the figure of Wisdom. We find in the sapiential Books of the Old Testament certain texts which exalt the role of Wisdom that existed prior to the world's creation. Passages such as the one from Psalm 90[89] should be interpreted in this sense: "Before the mountains were brought forth, or ever you had formed the earth and the world, from everlasting to everlasting you are God" (v. 2); or passages, like this one, that speak of the creator Wisdom: "The LORD created me at the beginning of his work, the first of his acts of old. Ages ago I was set up, at the first, before the beginning of the earth" (Prov 8:22–23). The praise of Wisdom, contained in the Book of the same name, is also evocative: "She reaches mightily from one end of the earth to the other, and she orders all things well" (Wis 8:1).

The sapiential texts themselves which speak of the eternal pre-existence of Wisdom, also speak of the descent, the abasement of this Wisdom, who pitched a tent for herself among men. Thus we already hear echoing the words of the Gospel of John, who speaks of the tent of the Lord's flesh. He created a tent for himself in the Old Testament: here the temple is shown, and worship in accordance with the Torah; but the New Testament perspective enables us to realize that this was only a prefiguration of the tent that was far more real and meaningful, the tent of Christ's flesh. And we already see in the Books of the Old Testament that this lowering of Wisdom, her descent in the flesh, also suggests the possibility that she was rejected. St. Paul, in developing his Christology, refers precisely to this sapiential perspective: in Jesus he recognizes the eternal wisdom that has always existed, the wisdom that descends and pitches a tent for herself among us and thus he can describe Christ as "the power of God and the wisdom of God" (1 Cor 1:24), he can say that Christ has become, through God's work, "our wisdom, our righteousness and sanctification and redemption" (1 Cor 1:30). Similarly, Paul explains that Christ, like Wisdom, can be rejected above all by the rulers of this world (cf. 1 Cor 2:6–9), so that within God's plans a paradoxical situation is created, the Cross, which was to transform itself into the means of salvation for the whole human race.

In the famous hymn contained in the Letter to the Philippians (cf. 2:6–11) a further development of this sapiential cycle sees Wisdom abase herself to then be exalted despite rejection. This is one of the most elevated texts in the whole of the New Testament. The vast majority of exegetes today agree that this passage reproduces an earlier composition than the text of the Letter to the Philippians. This is a very important fact because it means that Judeo-Christianity, prior to St. Paul, believed in Jesus' divinity. In other words, faith in the divinity of Jesus was not a Hellenistic invention that emerged much later than Jesus' earthly life, an invention which, forgetful of his humanity, would have divinized him; we see in reality that early Judeo-Christianity believed in the divinity of Jesus. Indeed, we can say that the Apostles themselves, at the important moments in the life of their Teacher, understood that he was the Son of God, as St. Peter said in Caesarea Philippi: "You are the Christ, the Son of the living God" (Mt 16:16).

However, let us return to the hymn in the Letter to the Philippians. This text's structure is in three strophes, which illustrate the high points on the journey undertaken by Christ. First, his pre-existence is expressed by the words, "Though he was in the form of God, he did not count equality with God a thing to be grasped" (Phil 2:6). Then comes the Son's voluntary self-abasement in the second strophe: ". . . but emptied himself, taking the form of a servant" (v. 7), to the point of humbling himself and "[becoming] obedient unto death, even death on a cross" (v. 8). The third strophe of the hymn proclaims the Father's response to the Son's humbling of himself: "Therefore God has highly exalted him and bestowed on him the name which is above every name" (v. 9). What is striking is the contrast between the radical humbling of himself and his subsequent glorification in the glory of God. It is obvious that this second strophe is in contrast with the claim of Adam, who wanted to make a God of himself, and in contrast with the act of the builders of the tower of Babel, who wanted to construct a bridge to heaven and make themselves divinities. However, this initiative of pride ended in self-destruction: this is not the way to heaven, to true happiness, to God. The gesture of the Son of God is exactly the opposite: not pride, but humility, which is the fulfillment of love, and love is divine. The initiative of Christ's abasement, of his radical humility, in stark contrast with human pride, is truly an expression of divine love; it is followed by that elevation into heaven to which God attracts us with his love.

In addition to the Letter to the Philippians, there are other places in Pauline literature where the themes of the pre-existence and descent to the earth of the Son of God are connected to each other. A reaffirmation of the assimilation of Wisdom and Christ, with all the connected cosmic and anthropological implications, is found in the First Letter to Timothy: "He was manifested in the flesh, vindicated in the Spirit, seen by angels, preached among the nations, believed on in the world, taken up in glory" (3:16). It is above all on these premises that a better definition of Christ as the sole Mediator is possible, against the background of the One God of the Old Testament (cf. 1 Tim 2:5 in relation to Is 43:10–11; 44:6). Christ is the true bridge that leads us to heaven, to communion with God.

And lastly, just a brief reference to the last developments of St. Paul's Christology in his Letters to the Colossians and to the Ephesians. In the former, Christ is described as the "first-born of all creation" (1:15). This word "first-born" suggests that the first of numerous children, the first of a great many brothers and sisters, came down to draw us and make us his brothers and sisters. In the Letter to the Ephesians we find a beautiful exposition of the *divine plan of salvation,* when Paul says that in Christ God desired to recapitulate everything (cf. Eph 1:23). Christ is the epitome of all things, he takes everything upon himself and guides us to God. And thus he involves us in a movement of descent and ascent, inviting us to share in his humility, that is, in his love for neighbor, in order also to share in his glorification, becoming with him sons in the Son. Let us pray the Lord to help us conform to his humility, to his love, in order to be rendered participants in his divinization.

CHAPTER TEN

The Importance of Christology:
The Theology of the Cross*

In the personal experience of St. Paul there is an incontrovertible factor: while he was at first a persecutor and perpetrated violence against Christians, from the moment of his conversion on the road to Damascus he switched to the side of the Crucified Christ, making Christ his *raison d'être* and the reason for his preaching. His was a life neither quiet nor free from dangers and difficulties, but spent entirely for souls (cf. 2 Cor 12:15). In his encounter with Jesus the central significance of the Cross had been made clear to him: he understood that Jesus *had died and risen for all* and for himself. Both these things were important: universality — Jesus really died for all; and subjectivity — he also died for me. Thus God's freely given and merciful love had been made manifest in the Cross. Paul experienced this love in himself first of all (cf. Gal 2:20) and from being a sinner he became a believer, from a persecutor an Apostle. Day after day, in his new life, he experienced that salvation was "grace," that everything derived from the death of Christ and not from his own merit, which moreover did not exist. The "Gospel of grace" thus became for him the only way of understanding the Cross, not only the criterion of his new existence but also his response to those who questioned him. First and foremost among these were the Jews who put their hope in deeds and from these hoped for salvation; then there were the

---

* General Audience, October 29, 2008.

Greeks who challenged the Cross with their human knowledge; lastly, there were those groups of heretics who had forged their own idea of Christianity to suit their own model of life.

For St. Paul the Cross has a fundamental primacy in the history of humanity; it represents the focal point of his theology because to say "Cross" is to say *salvation as grace* given to every creature. The topic of the Cross of Christ becomes an essential and primary element of the Apostle's preaching: the clearest example concerns the community of Corinth. Facing a Church in which disorder and scandal were disturbingly present, where communion was threatened by internal factions and ruptures which damaged the unity of the Body of Christ, Paul did not present himself with sublime words or wisdom but with the proclamation of Christ, of Christ Crucified. His strength is not in the use of persuasive language but, paradoxically, in the weakness and trepidation of those who entrust themselves solely to the "power of God" (cf. 1 Cor 2:1–5). The Cross, for all it represents, hence also for the theological message it contains, is scandal and folly. The Apostle says so with an impressive force that it is good to hear directly from his words: "For the word of the cross is folly to those who are perishing, but to us who are being saved it is the power of God. . . . It pleased God through the folly of what we preach to save those who believe. For Jews demand signs and Greeks seek wisdom, but we preach Christ crucified, a stumbling block to Jews and folly to Gentiles" (1 Cor 1:18–23).

The first Christian communities that Paul addressed knew well that Jesus was henceforth alive and risen; the Apostle does not only want to remind the Corinthians or the Galatians but also all of us that the Risen One is always the One who has been crucified. The "stumbling block" and "folly" of the Cross lie in the very fact that where there seems to be nothing but failure, sorrow, and defeat, there is the full power of God's boundless love, for the Cross is an expression of love, and love is the true power that is revealed precisely in this seeming weakness. For the Jews, the Cross is *skandalon,* that is, a snare or a stumbling block. It seems to hinder the faith of the devout Israelite who finds it difficult to discover anything like it in the Sacred Scriptures. With some courage, Paul seems to be saying that here the stakes at play are high: in the opinion of the Jews the Cross contradicts the very essence of God who manifested himself in wonderful signs. To accept the Cross of Christ therefore means bringing about a profound conversion in the way of relating to God. If, for the Jews, the reason for rejecting the Cross is found in Revelation, that is, the faithfulness to the God of the Fathers, for the Greeks, that is, the Gentiles, the criterion of judgment for opposing the Cross is reason. Indeed, the Cross for the latter is *moría,* folly, literally *ignorance,* that is, saltless food; thus, rather than an error, it is an insult to common sense.

Paul himself, on more than one occasion had the bitter experience of the rejection of the Christian proclamation, considered "insipid," devoid of importance, not even worthy of being taken into consideration at the level of rational logic. For those who, like the Greeks, see perfection in the spirit, in pure thought, it was already unacceptable that God should become man, immersing himself in all the limitations of space and time. Then for them it was definitely inconceivable to believe that a God could end on a Cross! And we see that this Greek logic is also the common logic of our time. How could the concept of *apátheia,* indifference, as an absence of passions in God, have understood a God who became man and was defeated, and was even to reassume his body subsequently to live as the Risen One? "We will hear you again about this" (Acts 17:32) the Athenians said scornfully to Paul when they heard him talking about the resurrection of the dead. They considered liberation from the body conceived as a prison as perfection. How could they not see the resumption of the body as an aberration? In ancient culture there did not seem to be room for the message of the Incarnate God. The entire "Jesus of Nazareth" event seemed to be marked by foolishness through and through, and the Cross was certainly its most emblematic point.

But why did St. Paul make precisely this, the work of the Cross, the fundamental core of his teaching? The answer is not difficult. The Cross reveals the power of God (cf. 1 Cor 1:24), which is different from human power. Indeed, it reveals his love: "For the foolishness of God is wiser than men, and the weakness of God is stronger than men" (1 Cor 1:25). Centuries after Paul we see that in history it was the Cross that triumphed and not the wisdom that opposed it. The Crucified One is wisdom, for he truly shows who God is, that is, a force of love which went even as far as the Cross to save men and women. God uses ways and means that seem to us at first sight to be merely weakness. The Crucified One reveals on the one hand man's frailty and on the other, the true power of God that is the free gift of love: this totally gratuitous love is true wisdom. St. Paul experienced this even in his flesh and tells us about it in various passages of his spiritual journey which have become precise reference points for every disciple of Jesus: "He said to me, 'My grace is sufficient for you, for my power is made perfect in weakness'" (2 Cor 12:9); and again "God chose what is weak in the world to shame the strong" (1 Cor 1:27). The Apostle identified so closely with Christ that in spite of being in the midst of so many trials, he too lived in the faith of the Son of God who loved him and gave himself for his sins and for the sins of all (cf. Gal 1:4; 2:20). This autobiographical fact concerning the Apostle becomes paradigmatic for all of us.

St. Paul gave a wonderful synthesis of the theology of the Cross in the Second Letter to the Corinthians (5:14–21) where everything is enclosed between two fundamental affirmations: on the one hand Christ, whom God made to be sin for our sake (v. 21), *he died for all* (v. 14); and on the other, God *reconciled us to himself* without imputing our sins to us (vv. 18–20). It is from this "ministry of reconciliation" that every form of slavery is already redeemed (cf. 1 Cor 6:20; 7:23). Here it appears how important this is for our lives. We too must enter into this "ministry of reconciliation" that always implies relinquishing one's superiority and opting for the folly of love.

St. Paul sacrificed his own life, devoting himself without reserve to the ministry of reconciliation, of the Cross, which is salvation for us all. And we too must be able to do this: may we be able to find our strength precisely in the humility of love and our wisdom in the weakness of renunciation, entering thereby into God's power. We must all model our lives on this true wisdom: we must not live for ourselves but must live in faith in that God of whom we can all say, "He loved me and gave himself for me."

CHAPTER ELEVEN

The Importance of Christology: The Decisiveness of the Resurrection*

"If Christ has not been raised, then our preaching is in vain and your faith is in vain . . . and you are still in your sins" (1 Cor 15:14–17). With these strong words from the First Letter to the Corinthians, St. Paul makes clear the decisive importance he attributes to the Resurrection of Jesus. In this event, in fact, lies the solution to the problem posed by the drama of the Cross. The Cross alone could not explain the Christian faith, indeed it would remain a tragedy, an indication of the absurdity of being. The Paschal Mystery consists in the fact that the Crucified man "was raised on the third day in accordance with the Scriptures" (1 Cor 15:4), as proto-Christian tradition attests. This is the keystone of Pauline Christology: everything rotates around this gravitational center. The whole teaching of Paul the Apostle starts *from,* and arrives *at,* the mystery of him whom the Father raised from the dead. The Resurrection is a fundamental fact, almost a prior axiom (cf. 1 Cor 15:12), on the basis of which Paul can formulate his synthetic proclamation (*kerygma*). He who was crucified and who thus manifested God's immense love for man, is risen again, and is alive among us.

It is important to understand the relationship between the proclamation of the Resurrection, as Paul formulates it, and that which was in use since the first pre-Pauline Christian communities. Here indeed we can see the importance of the tradition

---

* General Audience, November 5, 2008.

that preceded the Apostle and that he, with great respect and care, desires to pass on in his turn. The text on the Resurrection, contained in chapter 15:1–11 of the First Letter to the Corinthians, emphasizes the connection between "receiving" and "transmitting." St. Paul attributes great importance to the literal formulation of the tradition, and at the end of the passage under consideration underlines, "So we preach and so you believed" (1 Cor 15:11), so drawing attention to the oneness of the *kerygma,* of the proclamation for all believers and for those who will proclaim the Resurrection of Christ. The *tradition* to which he refers is the fount from which to draw. His Christology is never original at the expense of faithfulness to tradition. The *kerygma* of the Apostles always presides over the personal re-elaboration of Paul; each of his arguments moves from common tradition, and in them he expresses the faith shared by all the Churches, which are one single Church. In this way St. Paul offers a model for all time of how to approach theology and how to preach. The theologian, the preacher, does not create new visions of the world and of life, but he is at the service of truth handed down, at the service of the real fact of Christ, of the Cross, and of the Resurrection. His task is to help us understand today the reality of "God with us" that lies behind the ancient words, and thus the reality of true life.

We should here be explicit: St. Paul, in proclaiming the Resurrection, does not worry about presenting an organic doctrinal exposition; he does not wish to write what would effectively be a theological handbook, but he approaches the theme by replying to doubts and concrete questions asked of him by the faithful — an unprepared discourse, then, but one full of faith and theological experience. We find here a concentration of the essential: we have been "justified," that is, made just, saved, by Christ who *died* and *rose* again for us. Above all else the *fact* of the Resurrection emerges, without which Christian life would be simply in vain. On that Easter morning something extraordinary happened, something new, and at the same time very concrete, distinguished by very precise signs and recorded by numerous witnesses. For Paul, as for the other authors of the New Testament, the Resurrection is closely bound to the *testimony* of those who had direct experience of the Risen One. This means seeing and hearing, not only with the eyes or with the senses, but also with an interior light that assists the recognition of what the external senses attest as objective fact.

Paul gives, therefore, as do the four Gospels, primary importance to the theme of the *appearances*, which constitute a fundamental condition for belief in the Risen One who left the tomb empty. These two facts are important: *the tomb is empty* and *Jesus has in fact appeared.* In this way the links of that tradition were forged, which, through the testimony of the Apostles and the first disciples, was to reach successive generations until it came down to our own. The first consequence, or the first way of expressing this testimony, is to preach the Resurrection of Christ as a synthesis of the Gospel proclamation and as the culminating point in the salvific itinerary. Paul does all this on many occasions. Looking at the letters and the Acts of the Apostles, we can see that for him the essential point is to bear witness to the Resurrection. I should like to cite just one text: Paul, arrested in Jerusalem, stands accused before the Sanhedrin. In this situation, where his life is at stake, he indicates what is the sense and content of all his preaching, "With respect to the hope and the resurrection of the dead I am on trial" (Acts 23:6). This same phrase Paul continually repeats in his letters (cf. 1 Thess 1:9ff; 4:13–18; 5:10), in which he refers to his own personal experience, to his own meeting with the Risen Christ (cf. Gal 1:15–16, 1 Cor 9:1).

But we may wonder: What, for St. Paul, is the deep meaning of the Resurrection of Jesus? What has he to say to us across these 2,000 years? Is the affirmation "Christ is risen" relevant to us today? Why is the Resurrection so important, both for him and for us? Paul gives a solemn answer to this question at the beginning of his Letter to the Romans, where he begins by referring to "the gospel of God . . . concerning his Son, who was descended from David according to the flesh, and designated Son of God in power according to the spirit of holiness by his resurrection from the dead" (Rom 1:1–4). Paul knows well, and often says, that Jesus was always the Son of God, from the moment of his Incarnation. The novelty of the Resurrection consists in the fact that Jesus, raised from the lowliness of his earthly existence, is constituted Son of God "in power." Jesus, humiliated up to the moment of his death on the Cross, can now say to the Eleven, "All authority in heaven and on earth has been given to me" (Mt 28:18). The affirmation of Psalm 2:8 has come to pass. "Ask of me, and I will make the nations your heritage, and the ends of the earth your possession."

So, with the Resurrection begins the proclamation of the Gospel of Christ to all peoples; the Kingdom of Christ begins, this new Kingdom that knows no power other than that of truth and love. The Resurrection thus reveals definitively the real identity and the extraordinary stature of the Crucified One. An incomparable and towering dignity: *Jesus is God!* For St. Paul, the secret identity of Jesus is revealed even more in the mystery of the Resurrection than in the Incarnation. *While the title of Christ*, that is, "Messiah," "the Anointed," in St. Paul tends to become the proper name of Jesus, and that of "the *Lord*" indicates his personal relationship with believers, now the title "*Son of God*" comes to illustrate the intimate relationship of Jesus with God, a relationship which is fully revealed in the Paschal event. We can say, therefore, that Jesus rose again to be the Lord of the living and the dead (cf. Rom 14:9; 2 Cor 5:15), or in other words, our Savior (cf. Rom 4:25).

All this bears important consequences for our lives as believers: we are called upon to take part, in our inmost selves, in the whole story of the death and Resurrection of Christ. The Apostle says we "have died with Christ" and we believe we shall "live with him. For we know that Christ being raised from the dead, will never die again; death no longer has dominion over him" (Rom 6:8–9). This means sharing in the suffering of Christ, which is a prelude to that full unity with him through the resurrection that we hope for. This is also what happened to St. Paul, whose personal experience is described in the letters in tones as sorrowful as they are realistic, "That I may know him and the power of his resurrection, and may share his sufferings, becoming like him in his death, that if possible I may attain the resurrection from the dead" (Phil 3:10–11; cf. 2 Tim 2:8–12). The theology of the Cross is not a theory, it is the reality of Christian life. To live in the belief in Jesus Christ, to live in truth and love implies daily sacrifice, implies suffering. Christianity is not the easy road; it is, rather, a difficult climb, but one illuminated by the light of Christ and by the great hope that is born of him.

St. Augustine says: Christians are not spared suffering, indeed they must suffer a little more, because to live the faith expresses the courage to face in greater depth the problems that life and history present. But only in this way, through the experience of suffering, can we know life in its profundity, in its beauty, in the great hope born from Christ crucified and risen again. The believer, however, finds himself between two poles. On the one hand, the Resurrection, which in a certain sense is already present and operating within us (cf. Col 3:1–4; Eph 2:6); on the other, the urgency to enter into the process which leads everyone and everything towards that fullness described in the Letter to the Romans with a bold image: as the whole of Creation groans and suffers almost as with the pangs of childbirth, so we groan in the expectation of the redemption of our bodies, of our redemption and resurrection (cf. Rom 8:18–23).

In synthesis, we can say with Paul that the true believer obtains salvation by professing with his mouth that Jesus is the

Lord and believing in his heart that *God has raised Him from the dead* (cf. Rom 10:9). Important above all else is the heart that believes in Christ, and which in its faith "touches" the Risen One; but it is not enough to carry our faith in our hearts, we must confess it and bear witness to it with our mouths, with our lives, thus making the truth of the Cross and the Resurrection present in our history. In this way the Christian becomes part of that process by which the first Adam, a creature of the earth, and subject to corruption and death, is transformed into the last Adam, heavenly and incorruptible (cf. 1 Cor 15:20–22 and 42–49). This process was set in motion by the Resurrection of Christ, and it is, therefore, on this that we found our hope that we too may one day enter with Christ into our true homeland, which is in heaven. Borne up by this hope, let us continue with courage and with joy.

CHAPTER TWELVE

Eschatology: The Expectation
of the *Parousia**

The subject of the Resurrection on which we reflected in the last chapter unfolds a new perspective, that of the expectation of the Lord's return. It thus brings us to ponder on the relationship among the present time, the time of the Church and of the Kingdom of Christ, and the future (*éschaton*) that lies in store for us, when Christ will consign the Kingdom to his Father (cf. 1 Cor 15:24). Every Christian discussion of the last things, called eschatology, always starts with the event of the Resurrection; in this event the last things have already begun and, in a certain sense, are already present.

Very likely it was in the year 52 that St. Paul wrote the first of his letters, the First Letter to the Thessalonians, in which he speaks of this return of Jesus, called *Parousia* or *Advent,* his new, definitive, and manifest presence (cf. 4:13–18). The Apostle wrote these words to the Thessalonians who were beset by doubts and problems: "For since we believe that Jesus died and rose again, even so, through Jesus, God will bring with him those who have fallen asleep" (4:14). And Paul continues, "The dead in Christ will rise first; then we who are alive, who are left, shall be caught up together with them in the clouds to meet the Lord in the air; and so we shall always be with the Lord" (4:16–17). Paul describes Christ's *Parousia* in especially vivid tones and with symbolic imagery which, however, conveys a simple and profound

---

* General Audience, November 12, 2008.

message: we shall ultimately be with the Lord forever. Over and above the images, this is the essential message: our future is "to be with the Lord." As believers, we are already with the Lord in our lifetime; our future, eternal life, has already begun.

In his Second Letter to the Thessalonians, Paul changes his perspective. He speaks of the negative incidents that must precede the final and conclusive event. We must not let ourselves be deceived, he says, to think that, according to chronological calculations, the day of the Lord is truly imminent: "Now concerning the coming of our Lord Jesus Christ and our assembling to meet him, we beg you, brethren, not to be quickly shaken in mind or excited, either by spirit or by word, or by letter purporting to be from us, to the effect that the day of the Lord has come. Let no one deceive in any way" (2:1–3). The continuation of this text announces that before the Lord's arrival there will be apostasy, and one well described as the "man of lawlessness . . . the son of perdition" (2:3) must be revealed, who tradition would come to call the Antichrist. However, the intention of St. Paul's letter is primarily practical. He writes, "For even when we were with you, we we gave you this command: If any one will not work, let him not eat. For we hear that some of you are walking in idleness, mere busybodies, not doing any work. Now such persons we command and exhort in the Lord Jesus Christ to do their work in quietness and to earn their own living" (3:10–12). In other words, the expectation of Jesus' *Parousia* does not dispense us from working in this world but, on the contrary, creates responsibility to the divine Judge for our actions in this world. For this very reason our responsibility for working *in* and *for* this world increases. We shall see the same thing next Sunday in the Gospel of the Talents, in which the Lord tells us that he has entrusted talents to everyone and that the Judge will ask for an account of them, saying, "Have they been put to good use?" Hence the expectation of his return implies responsibility for this world.

The same thing and the same connection between *Parousia*—the return of the Judge/Savior—and our commitment in our lives appears in another context and with new aspects in the Letter to the Philippians. Paul is in prison, awaiting a sentence that might be condemnation to death. In this situation he is reflecting on his future existence with the Lord, but he is also thinking of the community of the Philippians who need their father, Paul, and he writes: "For me to live is Christ, and to die is gain. If it is to be life in the flesh, that means fruitful labor for me. Yet which I shall choose I cannot tell. I am hard pressed between the two. My desire is to depart and be with Christ, for that is far better. But to remain in the flesh is more necessary on your account. Convinced of this, I know that I shall remain and continue with you all, for your progress and joy in the faith, so that in me you may have ample cause to glory in Christ Jesus, because of my coming to you again" (1:21–26).

Paul has no fear of death; indeed, on the contrary, death indicates being totally with Christ. Yet Paul also shares in the sentiments of Christ who did not live for himself but for us. Living for others becomes his life and plan, thus demonstrates his perfect readiness to do God's will, to do whatever God decides. Above all he is prepared, in the future as well, to live on this earth for others, to live for Christ, to live for his living presence and thus for the renewal of the world. We see that his being with Christ creates a broad inner freedom: freedom in the face of the threat of death, but also freedom in the face of all life's commitments and sufferings. He is simply at God's disposal and truly free.

And now, after examining the various aspects of the expectation of Christ's *Parousia*, let us ask ourselves: What are the basic convictions of Christians as regards the last things — death, the end of the world? Their first conviction is the certainty that Jesus is Risen and is with the Father and thus is with us forever. And no one is stronger than Christ, for he is with the Father, he is with us. We are consequently safe, free of fear. This was an essential effect of Christian preaching. Fear of spirits and divinities was widespread in the ancient world. Today too, missionaries alongside many good elements in natural religions encounter fear of the spirits, of evil powers that threaten us. Christ lives, he has overcome death, he has overcome all these powers. We live in this certainty, in this freedom, and in this joy. This is the first aspect of our living with regard to the future.

The second is the certainty that Christ is with me. And just as the future world in Christ has already begun, this also provides the certainty of hope. The future is not darkness in which no one can find his way. It is not like that. Without Christ, even today the world's future is dark, and fear of the future is so common. Christians know that Christ's light is stronger, and therefore they live with a hope that is not vague, with a hope that gives them certainty and courage to face the future.

Lastly, their third conviction is that the Judge who returns at the same time as Judge and Savior has left us the duty to live in this world in accordance with his way of living. He has entrusted his talents to us. Our third conviction, therefore, is responsibility before Christ for the world, for our brethren, and at the same time also for the certainty of his mercy. Both these things are important. Since God can only be merciful we do not live as if good and evil were the same thing. This would be a deception. In reality, we live with a great responsibility. We have talents, and our responsibility is to work so that this world may be open to Christ, that it be renewed. Yet even as we work responsibly, we realize that God is the true Judge. We are also certain that this Judge is good; we know his Face, the Face of the Risen Christ, of Christ crucified for us. Therefore we can be certain of his goodness and advance with great courage.

Another element in the Pauline teaching on eschatology is the universality of the call to faith which unites Jews and Gentiles, that is, non-Christians as a sign and an anticipation of the future reality. For this reason we can say that we are already seated in heaven with Jesus Christ, but to reveal the riches of grace in the centuries to come (Eph 2:6f.), the *after* becomes a *before,* in order to show the state of incipient fulfillment in which we live. This makes bearable the sufferings of the present time which, in any case, cannot be compared to the future glory (cf. Rom 8:18). We walk by faith, not by sight, and even if we might rather leave the body to live with the Lord, what definitively matters, whether we are dwelling in the body or are far from it, is that we be pleasing to him (cf. 2 Cor 5:7–9).

Finally, a last point that might seem to us somewhat difficult. At the end of his First Letter to the Corinthians, St. Paul reiterates and also puts on the lips of the Corinthians a prayer that originated in the first Christian communities in the Palestinian area: *Maranà, thà!* which means literally, "Our Lord, come!" (16:22). It was the prayer of early Christianity and also of the last book of the New Testament, Revelation, which ends with it: "Come, Lord Jesus!" Can we pray like this too? It seems to me that for us today, in our lives, in our world, it is difficult to pray sincerely for the world to perish so that the new Jerusalem, the Last Judgment, and the Judge, Christ, may come. I think that even if, sincerely, we do not dare to pray like this for a number of reasons yet, in a correct and proper way, we too can say, together with the early Christians: "Come, Lord Jesus!" We do not of course desire the end of the world.

Nevertheless, we do want this unjust world to end. We also want the world to be fundamentally changed, we want the beginning of the civilization of love, the arrival of a world of justice and peace, without violence, without hunger. We want all this, yet how can it happen without Christ's presence? Without Christ's presence there will never be a truly just and renewed world. And even if we do so in a different way, we too can and must also say, completely and profoundly, with great urgency and amid the circumstances of our time: "Come, Lord Jesus! Come in your way, in the ways that you know. Come wherever there is injustice and violence. Come to the refugee camps, in Darfur, in North Kivu, in so many parts of the world. Come wherever drugs prevail. Come among those wealthy people who have forgotten you, who live for themselves alone. Come wherever you are unknown. Come in your way and renew today's world. And come into our hearts, come and renew our lives, come into our hearts so that we ourselves may become the light of God, your presence. In this way let us pray with St. Paul: *Maranà, thà!* "Come, Lord Jesus!" and let us pray that Christ may truly be present in our world today and renew it.

CHAPTER THIRTEEN

The Doctrine of Justification:
From Works to Faith*

On the journey we are making under St. Paul's guidance, let us now reflect on a topic at the center of the controversies of the century of the Reformation: the question of justification. How does man become just in God's eyes? When Paul met the Risen One on the road to Damascus he was an accomplished man; irreproachable according to the justice deriving from the Law (cf. Phil 3:6), Paul surpassed many of his contemporaries in the observance of the Mosaic Law and zealously upheld the traditions of his fathers (cf. Gal 1:14). The illumination of Damascus radically changed his life; he began to consider all merits acquired in an impeccable religious career as "refuse," in comparison with the sublimity of knowing Jesus Christ (cf. Phil 3:8). The Letter to the Philippians offers us a moving testimony of Paul's transition from a justice founded on the Law and acquired by his observance of the required actions, to a justice based on faith in Christ. He had understood that what until then had seemed to him to be a gain, before God was, in fact, a loss; and thus he had decided to stake his whole existence on Jesus Christ (cf. Phil 3:7). The treasure hidden in the field and the precious pearl for whose purchase all was to be invested were no longer a function of the Law, but Jesus Christ, his Lord.

The relationship between Paul and the Risen One became so deep as to induce him to maintain that Christ was no longer

---

* General Audience, November 19, 2008.

solely his life but also his very living, to the point that to be able to reach him death became a gain (cf. Phil 1:21). This is not to say he despised life, but that he realized that for him at this point there was no other purpose in life, and thus he had no other desire than to reach Christ as in an athletics competition and to remain with him forever. The Risen Christ had become the beginning and the end of his existence, the cause and the goal of his race. It was only his concern for the development in faith of those he had evange-lized and his anxiety for all of the Churches he founded (cf. 2 Cor 11:28) that induced him to slow down in his race towards his one Lord, to wait for his disciples so they might run with him towards the goal. Although from a perspective of moral integrity he had nothing to reproach himself in his former observance of the Law, once Christ had reached him he preferred not to make judgments on himself (cf. 1 Cor 4:3–4). Instead he limited himself to resolv-ing to press on, to make his own the One who had made him his own (cf. Phil 3:12).

It is precisely because of this personal experience of relation-ship with Jesus Christ that Paul henceforth places at the center of his Gospel an irreducible opposition between the two alterna-tive paths to justice: one built on the works of the Law, the other founded on the grace of faith in Christ. The alternative between justice by means of works of the Law and that by faith in Christ thus became one of the dominant themes that run through his letters: "We ourselves, who are Jews by birth and not Gentile sin-ners, yet who know that a man is not justified by works of the law but through faith in Jesus Christ, even we have believed in Christ Jesus in order to be justified by faith in Christ, and not by works of the law, because by works of the law no one will be justi-fied" (Gal 2:15–16). And to the Christians of Rome he reasserts that "all have sinned and fall short of the glory of God, they are justified by his grace as a gift, through the redemption which is in Christ Jesus" (Rom 3:23–24). And he adds, "We hold that a man is justified by faith apart from works of the law" (Rom 3:28). At this point Luther translated: "justified by faith alone." I shall return to this point at the end of the Catechesis. First, we must explain what is this "Law" from which we are freed and what are those "works of the Law" that do not justify. The opinion that was to recur systematically in history already existed in the community at Corinth. This opinion consisted in thinking that it was a question of moral law and that the Christian freedom thus consisted in the liberation from ethics. Thus in Corinth the term "πάντα μοι ἔξεστιν" (I can do what I like) was widespread. It is obvious that this interpretation is wrong: Christian freedom is not libertinism; the liberation of which St. Paul spoke is not liberation from good works.

So what does the Law from which we are liberated and which does not save mean? For St. Paul, as for all his contemporaries, the word "Law" meant the Torah in its totality, that is, the five books of Moses. The Torah, in the Pharisaic interpretation, that which Paul had studied and made his own, was a complex set of conduct codes that ranged from the ethical nucleus to observances of rites and worship, and that essentially determined the identity of the just person. In particular, these included circumcision, observances concerning pure food and ritual purity in general, the rules regarding the observance of the Sabbath, etc. — codes of conduct that also appear frequently in the debates between Jesus and his contemporaries. All of these observances that express a social, cultural, and religious identity had become uniquely important in the time of Hellenistic culture, starting from the third century B.C. This culture, which had become the universal culture of that time and was a seemingly rational culture — a polytheistic culture, seemingly tolerant — constituted a strong pressure for cultural uniformity and thus threatened the identity of Israel, which was politically constrained to enter into this common identity of the Hellenistic culture. This resulted in the loss of its own identity, hence also the loss of the precious heritage of the faith of the Fathers, of the faith in the one God and in the promises of God.

Against this cultural pressure, which not only threatened the Israelite identity but also the faith in the one God and in his promises, it was necessary to create a wall of distinction, a shield of defense to protect the precious heritage of the faith; this wall consisted precisely in the Judaic observances and prescriptions. Paul, who had learned these observances in their role of defending God's gift, of the inheritance of faith in one God alone, saw this identity threatened by the freedom of the Christians; this is why he persecuted them. At the moment of his encounter with the Risen One he understood that with Christ's Resurrection the situation had changed radically. With Christ, the God of Israel, the one true God, became the God of all peoples. The wall as he says in his Letter to the Ephesians between Israel and the Gentiles, was no longer necessary: it is Christ who protects us from polytheism and all of its deviations; it is Christ who unites us *with* and *in* the one God; it is Christ who guarantees our true identity within the diversity of cultures. The wall is no longer necessary; our common identity within the diversity of cultures is Christ, and it is he who makes us just. Being just simply means being with Christ and in Christ. And this suffices. Further observances are no longer necessary. For this reason Luther's phrase "*faith alone*" is true, if it is not opposed to faith in charity, in love. Faith is looking at Christ, entrusting oneself to Christ, being united to Christ, conformed to Christ, to his life. And the form, the life of Christ, is love; hence to believe is to conform to Christ and to enter into his love. So it is that in the Letter to the Galatians in which he primarily developed his teaching on justification St. Paul speaks of faith that works through love (cf. Gal 5:14).

Paul knows that in the twofold love of God and neighbor the whole of the Law is present and carried out. Thus in communion with Christ, in a faith that creates charity, the entire Law is ful-filled. We become just by entering into communion with Christ who is Love. We shall see the same thing in the Gospel next Sunday, the Solemnity of Christ the King. It is the Gospel of the judge whose sole criterion is love. What he asks is only this: Did you visit me when I was sick? When I was in prison? Did you give me food to eat when I was hungry, did you clothe me when I was naked? And thus justice is decided in charity. Thus, at the end of this Gospel we can almost say: love alone, charity alone. But there is no contradiction between this Gospel and St. Paul. It is the same vision, according to which communion with Christ, faith in Christ, creates charity. And charity is the fulfillment of communion with Christ. Thus, we are just by being united with him and in no other way.

At the end, we can only pray the Lord that he help us to believe; really believe. Believing thus becomes life, unity with Christ, the transformation of our life. And thus, transformed by his love, by the love of God and neighbor, we can truly be just in God's eyes.

CHAPTER FOURTEEN

The Doctrine of Justification: The Apostle's Teaching on Faith and Works[*]

In the last chapter I spoke of how man is justified before God. Following St. Paul, we have seen that man is unable to "justify" himself with his own actions, but can only truly become "just" before God because God confers his "justice" upon him, uniting him to Christ his Son. And man obtains this union through faith. In this sense, St. Paul tells us: not our deeds, but rather faith, renders us "just." This faith, however, is not a thought, an opinion, an idea. This faith is communion with Christ, which the Lord gives to us, and thus becomes life, becomes conformity with him. Or to use different words faith, if it is true, if it is real, becomes love, becomes charity, is expressed in charity. A faith without charity, without this fruit, would not be true faith. It would be a dead faith.

Thus, in the last chapter, we discovered two levels: that of the insignificance of our actions and of our deeds to achieve salvation, and that of "justification" through faith which produces the fruit of the Spirit. The confusion of these two levels has caused more than a few misunderstandings in Christianity over the course of centuries. In this context it is important that St. Paul, in the same Letter to the Galatians, radically accentuates, on the one hand, the freely given nature of justification that is not dependent on

---

[*] General Audience, November 26, 2008.

our works, but which at the same time also emphasizes the relationship between faith and charity, between faith and works: "In Christ Jesus neither circumcision nor uncircumcision is of any avail, but only faith working through love" (Gal 5:6). Consequently, there are on the one hand "works of the flesh," which are "immorality, impurity, licentiousness, idolatry" (Gal 5:19–20): all works that are contrary to the faith. On the other, there is the action of the Holy Spirit who nourishes Christian life, inspiring "love, joy, peace, patience, kindness, goodness, faithfulness, gentleness, self-control" (Gal 5:22–23). These are the fruits of the Spirit that blossom from faith.

Agape, love, is cited at the beginning of this list of virtues and self-control at the conclusion. In fact, the Spirit who is the Love of the Father and the Son pours out his first gift, *agape,* into our hearts (cf. Rom 5:5); and to be fully expressed, *agape,* love, requires self-control. In my first Encyclical, *Deus Caritas Est,* I also treated of the love of the Father and the Son which reaches us and profoundly transforms our existence. Believers know that reciprocal love is embodied in the love of God and of Christ, through the Spirit. Let us return to the Letter to the Galatians. Here St. Paul says that by bearing one another's burdens believers are fulfilling the commandment of love (cf. Gal 6:2).

Justified through the gift of faith in Christ, we are called to live in the love of Christ for neighbor, because it is on this criterion that we shall be judged at the end of our lives. In reality Paul only repeats what Jesus himself said and which is proposed to us anew by last Sunday's Gospel, in the parable of the Last Judgment. In the First Letter to the Corinthians St. Paul pours himself out in a famous eulogy of love. It is called the "hymn to love": "If I speak in the tongues of men and of angels, but have not love, I am a noisy gong or a clanging cymbal . . . Love is patient and kind; love is not jealous or boastful; it is not arrogant or rude. Love does not insist on its own way" (1 Cor 13:1, 4–5). Christian love is particularly demanding because it springs from Christ's total love for us: that love that claims us, welcomes us, embraces us, sustains us, to the point of tormenting us since it forces each one to no longer live for himself, closed into his own selfishness, but for him "who for their sake died and was raised" (2 Cor 5:15). The love of Christ makes us, in him, that new creation (cf. 2 Cor 5:17), which comes to belong to his Mystical Body that is the Church.

Seen in this perspective, the centrality of justification without works, the primary object of Paul's preaching, does not clash with faith that works through love; indeed, it demands that our faith itself be expressed in a life in accordance with the Spirit. Often there is seen an unfounded opposition between St. Paul's theology and that of St. James, who writes in his letter: "as the body apart from the spirit is dead, so faith apart from works is dead" (2:26). In reality, while Paul is primarily concerned to show that faith in Christ is necessary and sufficient, James accentuates the consequential relations between faith and works (cf. Jas 2:24). Therefore, for both Paul and James, faith that is active in love testifies to the freely given gift of justification in Christ. Salvation received in Christ needs to be preserved and witnessed to "with fear and trembling. For God is at work in you, both to will and to work for his good pleasure. . . . Do all things without grumbling or questioning . . . holding fast the word of life," St. Paul was to say further, to the Christians of Philippi (cf. Phil 2:12–14, 16).

We are often induced to fall into the same misunderstandings that characterized the community of Corinth; those Christians thought that since they had been freely justified in Christ through faith, "they could do as they pleased." And they believed, — and it often seems that today's Christians also think this — that it is permissible to create divisions in the Church, the Body of Christ, to celebrate the Eucharist without looking after the neediest of our brothers, to aspire to better *charisms* without being aware that each is a member of the other, and so forth. The consequences of a faith that is not manifested in love are disastrous, because it reduces itself to the arbitrariness and subjectivism that is most harmful to us and to our brothers. On the contrary, in following St. Paul, we should gain a new awareness of the fact that precisely because we are justified in Christ, we no longer belong to ourselves but have become a temple of the Spirit and hence are called to glorify God in our body with the whole of our existence (cf. 1 Cor 6:19). We would be underselling the inestimable value of justification, purchased at the high price of Christ's Blood, if we were not to glorify him with our body. In fact, our worship at the same time reasonable and spiritual is exactly this, which is why St. Paul exhorts us "to present [our] bodies as a living sacrifice, holy and acceptable to God" (Rom 12:1). To what would a liturgy be reduced if addressed solely to the Lord without simultaneously becoming service to one's brothers, a faith that would not express itself in charity? And the Apostle often places his communities in confrontation with the Last Judgment, on the occasion of which "we must all appear before the judgment seat of Christ, so that each one may receive good or evil, according to what he has done in the body" (2 Cor 5:10; cf. also Rom 2:16). And this idea of the Last Judgment must illumine us in our daily lives.

If the ethics that Paul proposes to believers do not deteriorate into forms of moralism, and if they prove themselves timely for us, it is because, each time, they start from the personal and communal relationship with Christ, to be realized concretely in a life according to the Spirit. This is essential: the Christian ethic is not born from a system of commandments but is a consequence of our friendship with Christ. This friendship influences life; if it is true it incarnates and fulfils itself in love for neighbor. For this reason, any ethical decay is not limited to the individual sphere but it also weakens personal and communal faith from which it derives and on which it has a crucial effect. Therefore let us allow ourselves to be touched by reconciliation, which God has given us in Christ, by God's "foolish" love for us; nothing and no one can ever separate us from his love (cf. Rom 8:39). We live in this certainty. It is this certainty that gives us the strength to live concretely the faith that works in love.

CHAPTER FIFTEEN

The Apostle's Teaching on the Relation between Adam and Christ[*]

In this chapter we shall reflect on the relation between Adam and Christ, defined by St. Paul in the well-known passage of the Letter to the Romans (5:12–21) in which he gives the Church the essential outline of the doctrine on original sin. Indeed, Paul had already introduced the comparison between our first progenitor and Christ while addressing faith in the Resurrection in the First Letter to the Corinthians: "For as in Adam all die, so also in Christ shall all be made alive. . . . 'The first man Adam became a living soul'; the last Adam became a life-giving spirit" (1 Cor 15:22, 45). With Romans 5:12–21, the comparison between Christ and Adam becomes more articulate and illuminating: Paul traces the history of salvation from Adam to the Law and from the latter to Christ. At the center of the scene it is not so much Adam, with the consequences of his sin for humanity, who is found, as much as it is Jesus Christ and the grace which was poured out on humanity in abundance through him. The repetition of the "all the more" with regard to Christ stresses that the gift received in him far surpasses Adam's sin and its consequent effects on humanity, so that Paul could reach his conclusion: "But where sin increased, grace abounded all the more" (Rom 5:20). The comparison that Paul draws between Adam and Christ therefore sheds light on

---

[*] General Audience, December 3, 2008.

the inferiority of the first man compared to the prevalence of the second.

On the other hand, it is precisely in order to highlight the immeasurable gift of grace in Christ that Paul mentions Adam's sin. One could say that if it were not to demonstrate the centrality of grace, he would not have dwelt on the treatment of sin which "came into the world through one man and death through sin" (Rom 5:12). For this reason, if, in the faith of the Church, an awareness of the dogma of original sin developed, it is because it is inseparably linked to another dogma, that of salvation and freedom in Christ. The consequence of this is that we must never treat the sin of Adam and of humanity separately from the salvific context, in other words, without understanding them within the horizon of justification in Christ.

However, as people of today we must ask ourselves: What is this original sin? What does St. Paul teach, what does the Church teach? Is this doctrine still sustainable today? Many think that in light of the history of evolution, there is no longer room for the doctrine of a first sin that then would have permeated the whole of human history. And, as a result, the matter of Redemption and of the Redeemer would also lose its foundation. Therefore, does original sin exist or not? In order to respond, we must distinguish between two aspects of the doctrine on original sin. There exists an empirical aspect, that is, a reality that is concrete, visible — I would say tangible to all — and an aspect of mystery concerning the ontological foundation of this event. The empirical fact is that a contradiction exists in our being. On the one hand every person knows that he must do good and intimately wants to do it. Yet at the same time he also feels the other impulse to do the contrary, to follow the path of selfishness and violence, to do only what pleases him, while also knowing that in this way he is acting against the good, against God, and against his neighbor. In his Letter to the Romans St. Paul expressed this contradiction in our being in this way: "I can will what is right, but I cannot do it. For I do not do the good I want, but I do the evil I do not want" (7:18–19). This inner contradiction of our being is not a theory. Each one of us experiences it every day. And above all we always see around us the prevalence of this second will. It is enough to think of the daily news of injustice, violence, falsehood, and lust. We see it every day. It is a fact.

As a consequence of this evil power in our souls, a murky river developed in history which poisons the geography of human history. Blaise Pascal, the great French thinker, spoke of a "second nature," which superimposes our original, good nature. This "second nature" makes evil appear normal to man. Hence even the common expression "he's human" has a double meaning. "He's human," can mean, "This man is good, he really acts as one should act." But, "He's human," can also imply falsity: evil is normal, it is human. Evil seems to have become our second nature. This contradiction of the human being, of our history, must evoke, and still evokes today, the desire for redemption. And, in reality, the desire for the world to be changed and the promise that a world of justice, peace, and good will be created exists everywhere. In politics, for example, everyone speaks of this need to change the world, to create a more just world. And this is precisely an expression of the longing for liberation from the contradiction we experience within us.

Thus, the existence of the power of evil in the human heart and in human history is an undeniable fact. The question is: How can this evil be explained? In the history of thought, Christian faith aside, there exists a key explanation of this duality, with different variations. This model says that being in itself is contradictory, it bears within it both good and evil. In antiquity, this idea implied the opinion that two equally primal principles existed: a good principle and a bad principle. This duality would be insuperable; the two principles are at the same level, so this contradiction from the being's origin would always exist. The contradiction of our being would therefore only reflect the contrary nature of the two divine principles, so to speak. In the evolutionist, atheist version of the world the same vision returns in a new form. Although in this conception the vision of being is monist, it supposes that being as such bears within itself both evil and good from the outset. Being itself is not simply good, but open to good and to evil. Evil is equally primal with the good. And human history would develop only the model already present in all of the previous evolution. What Christians call original sin would in reality be merely the mixed nature of being, a mixture of good and evil which, according to atheist thought, belongs to the same fabric of being. This is a fundamentally desperate view: if this is the case, evil is invincible. In the end all that counts is one's own interest. All progress would necessarily be paid for with a torrent of evil and those who wanted to serve progress would have to agree to pay this price. Politics is fundamentally structured on these premises and we see the effects of this. In the end, this modern way of thinking can create only sadness and cynicism.

And let us therefore ask again: What does faith witnessed to by St. Paul tell us? As the first point, it confirms the reality of the competition between the two natures, the reality of this evil whose shadow weighs on the whole of Creation. We heard chapter seven of the Letter to the Romans; we shall add chapter eight. Quite simply, evil exists. As an explanation, in contrast with the dualism and monism that we have briefly considered and found distressing, faith tells us: there exist two mysteries, one of light and one of night (that is, however, enveloped by the mysteries of light). The first mystery of light is this: faith tells us that there are not two principles, one good and one evil, but there is only one single principle, God the Creator, and this principle is good, only good, without a shadow of evil. And therefore, being too is not a mixture of good and evil; being as such is good and therefore it is good to be, it is good to live. This is the good news of the faith: only one good source exists, the Creator. Therefore living is a good, it is a good thing to be a man or a woman, life is good. Then follows a mystery of darkness, or night. Evil does not come from the source of being itself, it is not equally primal. Evil comes from a freedom created, from a freedom abused.

How was it possible? How did it happen? This remains obscure. Evil is not logical. Only God and good are logical, are light. Evil remains mysterious. It is presented as such in great images, as it is in chapter 3 of Genesis, with that scene of the two trees, of the serpent, of sinful man: a great image that makes us guess but cannot explain what is itself illogical. We may guess, not explain; nor may we recount it as one fact beside another, because it is a deeper reality. It remains a mystery of darkness, of night. But a mystery of light is immediately added. Evil comes from a subordinate source. God with his light is stronger. And therefore evil can be overcome. Thus the creature, man, can be healed. The dualist visions, including the monism of evolution-ism, cannot say that man is curable; but if evil comes only from a subordinate source, it remains true that man is healable. And the Book of Wisdom says: "He made the nations of the world curable" (1:14, *Vulgate*). And finally, the last point: man is not only healable, but is healed de facto. God introduced healing. He entered into history in person. He set a source of pure good against the permanent source of evil. The Crucified and Risen Christ, the new Adam, counters the murky river of evil with a river of light. And this river is present in history: we see the saints, the great saints, but also the humble saints, the simple faithful. We see that the stream of light which flows from Christ is pres-ent, is strong.

CHAPTER SIXTEEN

Theology of the Sacraments[*]

In following St. Paul, we saw two things in the last chapter. The first is that our human history has been polluted from the outset by the misuse of created freedom which seeks emancipation from the divine Will. Thus, it does not find true freedom but instead opposes truth and consequently falsifies our human realities. It falsifies above all the fundamental relationships: with God, between a man and a woman, between humankind and the earth. We said that this contamination permeates the whole fabric of our history and that this hereditary defect has continued to spread within it and can now be seen everywhere. This was the first thing. The second is this: we have learned from St. Paul that a new beginning exists *in* history and *of* history in Jesus Christ, the One who is man and God. With Jesus, who comes from God, a new history begins that is shaped by his "yes" to the Father and is therefore not founded on the pride of a false emancipation but on love and truth.

However, the question now arises: How can we enter this new beginning, this new history? How does this new history reach me? We are inevitably linked to the first, contaminated history through our biological descendance, since we all belong to the one body of humanity; but how is communion with Jesus, how is new birth achieved in order to enter into the new humanity? How does Jesus come into my life, into my being? The fundamental response of St. Paul and of the whole of the New Testament is that he comes through the action of the Holy Spirit. If the first

---

[*] General Audience, December 10, 2008.

history starts, so to speak, with biology, the second starts with the Holy Spirit, the Spirit of the Risen Christ. At Pentecost this Spirit created the beginning of the new humanity, the new community, the Church, the Body of Christ.

However, we must be even more concrete: How can this Spirit of Christ, the Holy Spirit, become my Spirit? The answer is that this happens in three ways that are closely interconnected. This is the first: the Spirit of Christ knocks at the door of my heart, moves me from within. However, since the new humanity must be a true body, since the Spirit must gather us together and really create a community, since overcoming divisions and creating a gathering of the dispersed is characteristic of the new beginning, this Spirit of Christ uses two elements visibly aggregated: the Word of the proclamation and the sacraments, Baptism and the Eucharist in particular. In his Letter to the Romans, St. Paul says: "If you confess with your lips that Jesus is Lord and believe in your heart that God raised him from the dead, you will be saved" (10:9). In other words, you will enter the new history, a history of life and not of death. St. Paul then continues: "But how are men to call upon him in whom they have not believed? And how are they to believe in him of whom they have never heard? And how are they to hear without a preacher? And how can men preach unless they are sent?" (Rom 10:14–15). In an ensuing passage he says further: "Faith comes from what is heard" (Rom 10:17). Faith is not a product of our thought or our reflection; it is something new that we cannot invent but only receive as a gift, as a new thing produced by God. Moreover, faith does not come from reading but from listening. It is not only something interior but also a relationship with Someone. It implies an encounter with the proclamation; it implies the existence of the Other, who it proclaims, and creates communion.

And lastly, proclamation: the one who proclaims does not speak on his own behalf but is sent. He fits into a structure of mission that begins with Jesus, sent by the Father, passes through the Apostles (the term "Apostles" means "those who are sent") and continues in the ministry, in the missions passed down by the Apostles. The new fabric of history takes shape in this structure of missions in which we ultimately hear God himself speaking; his personal Word, the Son speaks with us, reaches us. The Word was made flesh, Jesus, in order really to create a new humanity. The word of proclamation thus becomes a sacrament in Baptism, which is rebirth from water and the Spirit, as St. John was to say. In the sixth chapter of the Letter to the Romans, St. Paul speaks of Baptism in a very profound way. We have heard the text but it might be useful to repeat it: "Do you not know that all of us who have been baptized into Christ Jesus were baptized into his death? We were buried therefore with him by Baptism into death, so that as Christ was raised from the dead by the glory of the Father, we too might walk in newness of life" (6:3–4).

In this Catechesis I cannot, of course, enter into a detailed interpretation of this far-from-easy text. I would like to note briefly just three points. The first: "We have been baptized," is a passive. No one can baptize himself, he needs the other. No one can become Christian on his own. Becoming Christian is a passive process. Only by another can we be made Christians, and this "other" who makes us Christians, who gives us the gift of faith, is in the first instance the community of believers, the Church. From the Church we receive faith, Baptism. Unless we let ourselves be formed by this community we do not become Christians. An autonomous, self-produced Christianity is a contradiction in itself. In the first instance, this "other" is the community of believers, the Church, yet in the second instance this community does not act on its own either, according to its own ideas and desires. The community also lives in the same passive process: Christ alone can constitute the Church. Christ is the true giver of the sacraments. This is the first point: no one baptizes himself, no one makes himself a Christian. We become Christians.

This is the second point: Baptism is more than a cleansing. It is death and resurrection. Paul himself, speaking in the Letter to the Galatians of the turning point in his life brought about by his encounter with the Risen Christ, describes it with the words: I am dead. At that moment a new life truly begins. Becoming Christian is more than a cosmetic operation that would add something beautiful to a more or less complete existence. It is a new beginning, it is rebirth: death and resurrection. Obviously in the resurrection what was good in the previous existence reemerges.

The third point is: matter is part of the sacrament. Christianity is not a purely spiritual reality. It implies the body. It implies the cosmos. It is extended toward the new earth and the new heavens. Let us return to the last words of St. Paul's text. In this way he said, "we too might walk in newness of life." It constitutes an examination of conscience for all of us: to walk in newness of life. This applies to Baptism.

We now come to the Sacrament of the Eucharist. I have already shown in other Catecheses the profound respect with which St. Paul transmits verbally the tradition of the Eucharist which he received from the witnesses of the last night themselves. He passes on these words as a precious treasure entrusted to his fidelity. Thus we really hear in these words the witnesses of the last night. We heard the words of the Apostle: "For I received from the Lord what I also delivered to you, that the Lord Jesus on the night when he was betrayed took bread, and when he had given thanks, he broke it, and said, 'This is my body which is for you. Do this in remembrance of me.' In the same way also the chalice, after supper, saying, 'This chalice is the new covenant in my blood. Do this, as often as you drink it, in remembrance of me'" (1 Cor 11:23–25). It is an inexhaustible text.

Here too, I have only two brief points to make. Paul transmits the Lord's words on the cup like this: this cup is "the new covenant in my Blood." These words conceal an allusion to two fundamental texts of the Old Testament. The first refers to the promise of a new covenant in the Book of the Prophet Jeremiah. Jesus tells the disciples and tells us: now, at this moment, with me and with my death the new covenant is fulfilled; by my Blood this new history of humanity begins in the world. However, also present in these words is a reference to the moment of the covenant on Sinai, when Moses said: "Behold the blood of the covenant which the LORD has made with you in accordance with all these words" (Ex 24:8). Then it was the blood of animals. The blood of animals could only be the expression of a desire, an expectation of the true sacrifice, the true worship. With the gift of the cup, the Lord gives us the true sacrifice. The one true sacrifice is the love of the Son. With the gift of this love, eternal love, the world enters into the new covenant. Celebrating the Eucharist means that Christ gives us himself, his love, to configure us to himself and thereby to create the new world.

The second important aspect of the teaching on the Eucharist appears in the same First Letter to the Corinthians where St. Paul says: "The cup of blessing which we bless, is it not a participation in the blood of Christ? The bread which we break, is it not a participation in the body of Christ? Because there is one bread, we who are many are one body, for we all partake of the one bread" (10:16–17). In these words, the personal and social character of the Sacrament of the Eucharist likewise appears. Christ personally unites himself with each one of us, but Christ himself is also united with the man and the woman who are next to me. And the bread is for me but it is also for the other. Thus Christ unites all of us with himself and all of us with one another. In communion we receive Christ. But Christ is likewise united with my neighbor: Christ and my neighbor are inseparable in the Eucharist. And thus we are all one bread and one body. A Eucharist without solidarity with others is a Eucharist abused. And here we come to the root and, at the same time, the kernel of the doctrine on the Church as the Body of Christ, of the Risen Christ.

We also perceive the full realism of this doctrine. Christ gives us his Body in the Eucharist, he gives himself in his Body and thus makes us his Body, he unites us with his Risen Body. If man eats ordinary bread, in the digestive process this bread becomes part of his body, transformed into a substance of human life. But in holy Communion the inverse process is brought about. Christ, the Lord, assimilates us into himself, introducing us into his glorious Body, and thus we all become his Body. Whoever reads only chapter 12 of the First Letter to the Corinthians and chapter 12 of the Letter to the Romans might think that the words about the Body of Christ as an organism of *charisms* is only a sort of sociological and theological parable. Actually in Roman political science this parable of the body with various members that form a single unit was used referring to the state itself, to say that the state is an organism in which each one has his role, that the multiplicity and diversity of functions form one body and each one has his place. If one reads only chapter 12 of the First Letter to the Corinthians one might think that Paul limited himself to transferring this alone to the Church, that here too it was solely a question of a sociology of the Church. Yet, bearing in mind this chapter 10, we see that the realism of the Church is something quite different, far deeper and truer than that of a state organism. Because Christ really gives his Body and makes us his Body. We really become united with the Risen Body of Christ and thereby are united with one another. The Church is not only a corporation like the state is, she is a body. She is not merely an organization but a real organism.

Lastly, just a very brief word on the Sacrament of Matrimony. In the Letter to the Corinthians there are only a few references whereas in the Letter to the Ephesians he has truly developed a profound theology of Matrimony. Here Paul defines Matrimony as a "great mystery." He says so "in reference to Christ and the Church" (5:32). A reciprocity in a vertical dimension should be pointed out in this passage. Mutual submission must use the language of love whose model is Christ's love for the Church. This Christ-Church relationship makes the theological aspect of matrimonial love fundamental, exalting the affective relationship between the spouses. A genuine marriage will be well lived if in the constant human and emotional growth an effort is made to remain continually bound to the efficacy of the Word and to the meaning of Baptism. Christ sanctified the Church, purifying her through the washing with water, accompanied by the Word. Apart from making it visible, a participation in the Body and Blood of the Lord does no more than seal a union rendered indissoluble by grace.

And lastly let us listen to St. Paul's words to the Philippians: "The Lord is at hand" (Phil 4:5). It seems to me that we have understood that the Lord is close to us throughout our life through the Word and through the sacraments. Let us pray that by his closeness we may always be moved in the depths of our being so that joy may be born, that joy which is born when Jesus really is at hand.

CHAPTER SEVENTEEN

Spiritual Worship*

The commitment of union with Christ is the example that St. Paul offers us. Continuing the Catecheses dedicated to him, let us pause to reflect on one of the important aspects of his thought which concerns the worship that Christians are called to exercise. In the past, it was fashionable to speak of a rather anti-religious tendency in the Apostle, of a "spiritualization" of the idea of worship. Today we understand better that Paul sees in the Cross of Christ a historic turning point that radically transforms and renews the reality of worship. In particular, there are three texts in the Letter to the Romans in which this new vision of worship appears.

1. In Romans 3:25, after speaking of the "redemption which is in Christ Jesus," Paul continues with what to us is a mysterious formula, saying: "Through his blood, God made him the means of expiation for all who believe." With these words that we find somewhat strange, "means of expiation," St. Paul mentions the so-called "propitiatory" of the ancient temple, that is, the lid covering the Ark of the Covenant that was considered the point of contact between God and man, the point of his mysterious presence in the human world. On the great Day of Atonement, *Yom Kippur*, this "proprietary" was sprinkled with the blood of sacrificed animals, blood that symbolically brought the sins of the past year into contact with God, and thus sins cast into the abyss of divine goodness were, so to speak, absorbed by the power of God, overcome and forgiven. Life began anew.

---

* General Audience, January 7, 2009.

St. Paul mentions this rite and says: This rite was an expression of the desire truly to be able to cast all our sins into the abyss of divine mercy and thus make them disappear. With the blood of animals, however, this expiation was not achieved; a more real contact between human sin and divine love was required. This contact took place on the Cross of Christ. Christ, the true Son of God, who became a true man, took all our sins upon himself. He himself is the point of contact between human wretchedness and divine mercy. In his heart the grievous mass of the evil perpetrated by humanity is dissolved and life is renewed.

In revealing this change, St. Paul tells us: the old form of worship with animal sacrifices in the Temple of Jerusalem ended with the Cross of Christ, the supreme act of divine love become human love. This symbolic worship, the cult of desire, is now replaced by true worship: the love of God incarnate in Christ and brought to its fulfillment in his death on the Cross. This is not, therefore, a spiritualization of true worship; on the contrary it is true worship: real divine-human love replaces the symbolic and temporary form of worship. The Cross of Christ, his love with Flesh and Blood, is the true worship that corresponds with the realities of God and of man. In Paul's opinion, the epoch of the temple and its worship had already ended prior to the external destruction of the temple. Here Paul finds himself in perfect harmony with the words of Jesus who had predicted the destruction of the temple and had also announced another temple, "not made with human hands," the temple of his Risen Body (cf. Mk 14:58; Jn 2:19ff.). This is the first text.

2. The second text I would like to speak of today is found in the first verse of chapter 12 of the Letter to the Romans. We have heard it, and I shall repeat it: "I appeal to you therefore, brethren, by the mercies of God, to present your bodies as a living sacrifice, holy and acceptable to God, which is your spiritual worship." There is an apparent paradox in these words: while the

sacrifice normally requires the *death* of the victim, Paul speaks on the contrary of the *life* of the Christian. The expression, "present your bodies," independently of the successive concept of sacrifice acquires the religious nuance of "giving as an oblation, an offering." The exhortation, "present your bodies," refers to the person in his entirety; in fact, in Romans 6:13, he invites them to: "yield yourselves." Moreover the explicit reference to the physical dimension of the Christian coincides with the invitation to: "glorify God in your body" (1 Cor 6:20). In other words, it is a question of honoring God in the most practical form of daily life that consists of relational and perceptible visibility.

Conduct of this kind is described by Paul as "a living sacrifice, holy and acceptable to God." It is here that we actually find the word "sacrifice." In this usage the term belongs to a sacred context and serves to designate the slaughtering of an animal, part of which can be burned in honor of the gods and another part eaten at a banquet by those who are offering the sacrifice. Paul applies it instead to the Christian's life. In fact, he describes this sacrifice using three adjectives. The first "living" expresses vitality. The second "holy" recalls the Pauline idea of holiness not linked to places or objects but to Christians themselves. The third "acceptable to God" recalls perhaps the recurrent biblical expression of sacrifice as "a pleasing odor" (cf. Lev 1:13, 17; 23:18; 26:31, etc.).

Immediately afterwards, Paul thus defines this new way of living, "which is your spiritual worship." Commentators on this text well know that the Greek expression (*ten logiken latreían*) is not easy to translate. The Latin Bible translates it as: "*rationabile obsequium.*" The actual word "*rationabile*" appears in the First Eucharistic Prayer of the Roman Canon: in it the faithful pray that God will accept this offering as "*rationabile.*" The usual Italian translation "*culto spirituale*" [spiritual worship] does not reflect all the nuances of the Greek text (or of the Latin). In any case it is not a matter of less real worship, or even worship that is only metaphorical, but rather of a more concrete and realistic worship, a worship in which the human being himself, in his totality as a being endowed with reason, becomes adoration, glorification of the living God.

This Pauline formula, which returns later in the Roman Eucharistic Prayer, is the fruit of a long development of the religious experience in the centuries before Christ. In this experience theological developments of the Old Testament and trends of Greek thought are encountered. I would like at least to show some elements of this development. The prophets and many Psalms strongly criticize the bloody sacrifices of the temple. Psalm 50[49], in which God speaks: "If I were hungry, I would not tell you; for the world and all that is in it is mine. Do I eat the flesh of bulls, or drink the blood of goats? Offer to God a sacrifice of thanksgiving" (vv. 12–14). The following Psalm says something similar: "You take no delight in sacrifice; were I to give a burnt offering, you would not be pleased. The sacrifice acceptable to God is a broken spirit; a broken and contrite heart, O God, you will not despise" (Ps 51[50]:16ff). In the Book of Daniel, at the time of the new destruction of the temple by the Hellenistic regime (second century B.C.), we find a new step in the same direction. In the heart of the furnace, that is, of persecution, suffering Azariah prays in these words: "And at this time there is no prince, or prophet, or leader, no burnt offering, or sacrifice, or oblation, or incense, no place to make an offering before you or to find mercy. Yet with a contrite heart and a humble spirit may we be accepted, as though it were with burnt offerings of rams and bulls . . . such may our sacrifice be in your sight this day, and may we wholly follow you" (Dan 3:15–17). In the destruction of the shrine and of worship, in this situation of the privation of any sign of God's presence, the believer offers as a true holocaust his contrite heart, his desire for God.

We see an important and beautiful development, but with a danger. There is a spiritualization, a moralization of worship: worship becomes only something of the heart, of the mind. But it lacks the body, it lacks the community. Thus we understand, for example, that Psalm 51, and also the Book of Daniel, despite the criticism of worship, desire a return to the time of sacrifices. Yet this is a renewed time, a renewed sacrifice, in a synthesis that was not yet foreseeable, that could not yet be conceived of.

Let us return to St. Paul. He is heir to these developments, of the desire for true worship, in which man himself becomes the glory of God, living adoration with his whole being. In this sense he says to the Romans: "Present your bodies as a living sacrifice . . . which is your spiritual worship" (Rom 12:1). Paul thus repeats what he pointed out in chapter 3: the time of animal sacrifices, substitute sacrifices, is over. The time has come for true worship. However, here there is also the danger of a misunderstanding. One might easily interpret this new worship in a moralistic sense: in offering our lives, we ourselves become true worship. In this way, worship with animals would be replaced by moralism: man himself would do everything on his own with his moral strength. And this was certainly not St. Paul's intention. However, the question remains: How, therefore, can we interpret this "[reasonable] spiritual worship"? Paul always presumes that we are all "one in Christ Jesus" (Gal 3:28), that we died in Baptism (cf. Rom 1), and that we now live with Christ, for Christ, in Christ.

In this union and only in this way we are able to become in him and with him "a living sacrifice," to offer "true worship." The sacrificed animals were meant to replace the human being, the gift of self, but they could not. In his gift of himself to the Father and to us, Jesus Christ is not a substitute, but truly bears within him the human being, our sins and our desires; he really represents us, he takes us upon himself. In communion with Christ, realized in faith and in the sacraments, despite all our inadequacies we truly become a living sacrifice: "true worship" is achieved.

This synthesis forms the background of the Roman Canon in which we pray for this offering to become *"rationabile,"* for spiritual worship to be made. The Church knows that in the Holy Eucharist Christ's gift of himself, his true sacrifice, becomes present. However, the Church prays that the community celebrating may truly be united with Christ and transformed; she prays that we may become what we cannot be with our own efforts: a "rational" offering that is acceptable to God. Thus the Eucharistic Prayer interprets St. Paul's words correctly. St. Augustine explained all this marvelously in the 10th chapter of his *City of God.* I cite only two sentences from it.

"This is the sacrifice of Christians: we, being many, are one body in Christ . . . The whole redeemed city, that is to say, the congregation or community of the saints, is offered to God as our sacrifice through the great High Priest, who offered Himself" (10, 6: *CCL* 47, 27 ff.).

3. Further, at the end, I add just a few words on the third text of the Letter to the Romans on the new worship. St. Paul thus said in chapter 15: "The grace given me by God to be a minister of Christ Jesus to the Gentiles in the priestly service [*hierourgein*] of the Gospel of God, so that the offering of the Gentiles may be acceptable, sanctified by the Holy Spirit" (15:15–16). I would like to emphasize only two aspects of this marvelous text, with regard to the unique terminology in the Pauline letters. First of all, St. Paul interprets his missionary activity among the world's peoples to build the universal Church as priestly service. To proclaim the Gospel in order to unite the peoples in the communion of the Risen Christ is a "priestly" action. The Apostle of the Gospel is a true priest, he does what is central to the priesthood: prepares the true sacrifice. And then the second aspect: the goal of missionary action is, we can say, the cosmic liturgy: that the peoples united in Christ, the world, may as such become the glory of God, an "acceptable [offering], sanctified by the Holy Spirit." Here the

dynamic aspect appears, the aspect of hope in the Pauline conception of worship: Christ's gift of himself implies the aspiration
to attract all to communion in his body, to unite the world. Only
in communion with Christ, the exemplary man, one with God,
does the world thus become as we all wish it to be: a mirror of
divine love. This dynamism is ever present in the Eucharist; this
dynamism must inspire and form our life.

CHAPTER EIGHTEEN

Letters to the Colossians
and Ephesians[*]

In St. Paul's correspondence there are two letters — to the Colossians and to the Ephesians — that to a certain extent can be considered twins. In fact, they both contain expressions that are found in them alone, and it has been calculated that more than a third of the words in the Letter to the Colossians are also found in the Letter to the Ephesians. For example, while in Colossians we read literally the invitation, "admonish one another in all wisdom, and as you sing psalms and hymns and spiritual songs with thankfulness in your hearts" (Col 3:16), in his Letter to the Ephesians St. Paul likewise recommends "addressing one another in psalms and hymns and spiritual songs, singing and making melody to the Lord with all your heart" (Eph 5:19). We could meditate upon these words: the heart must sing with psalms and hymns and the voice in the same way, in order to enter the tradition of prayer of the whole of the Church of the Old and New Testaments. Thus we learn to be with ourselves and one another and with God. In addition, the "domestic code" that is absent in the other Pauline letters is found in these two in other words, a series of recommendations addressed to husbands and wives, to parents and children, to masters and slaves (cf. Col 3:18—4:1 and Eph 5:22—6:9 respectively).

---

[*] General Audience, January 14, 2009.

It is even more important to notice that only in these two letters is the title "head" (*kefalé*) given to Jesus Christ. And this title is used on two levels. In the first sense, Christ is understood as head of the Church (cf. Col 2:18–19 and Eph 4:15–16). This means two things: first of all that he is the governor, the leader, the person in charge who guides the Christian community as its leader and Lord (cf. Col 1:18: "He is the head of the body, the Church"). The other meaning is then that, as head, he innervates and vivifies all the members of the body that he controls. (In fact, according to Colossians 2:19, it is necessary "[to hold] fast to the Head, from whom the whole body, [is] nourished and knit together"). That is, he is not only one who commands but also one who is organically connected with us, from whom comes the power to act in an upright way.

In both cases, the Church is considered subject to Christ, both in order to follow his supervision in the commandments and to accept all of the vital influences that emanate from him. His commandments are not only words or orders but a vital energy that comes from him and helps us.

This idea is developed particularly in Ephesians where, instead of being traced back to the Spirit (as in 1 Corinthians 12), even the ministries of the Church are conferred by the Risen Christ. It is he who established "that some should be apostles, some prophets, some evangelists, some pastors and teachers" (4:11). And it is from him that "the whole body, joined and knit together by every joint with which it is supplied . . . upbuilds itself in love" (4:16). Christ, in fact, fully strives to "present the church to himself in splendor, without spot or wrinkle or any such thing" (Eph 5:27). In saying this he tells us that the power with which he builds the Church, with which he guides the Church, with which he also gives the Church the right direction is precisely his love.

The first meaning is therefore Christ, Head of the Church; both with regard to her direction and, above all, with regard to her inspiration and organic revitalization by virtue of his love. Then, in a second sense, Christ is not only considered as head of the Church but also as head of the heavenly powers and of the entire cosmos. Thus, in Colossians, we read that Christ has "disarmed the principalities and powers and made a public example of them, triumphing over them in him" (2:15). Similarly, in Ephesians we find it written that with his Resurrection God placed Christ "far above all rule and authority and power and dominion, and above every name that is named, not only in this age but also in that which is to come" (1:21). With these words the two letters bring us a highly positive and fruitful message. It is this: Christ has no possible rival to fear since he is superior to every form of power that might presume to humble man. He alone "loved us and gave himself up for us" (Eph 5:2). Thus, if we are united with Christ, we have no enemy or adversity to fear; but this therefore means that we must continue to cling firmly to him, without loosening our grip!

For the pagan world that believed in a world filled with spirits for the most part dangerous and from which it was essential to protect oneself, the proclamation that Christ was the only conqueror and that those with Christ need fear no one seemed a true liberation. The same is also true for the paganism of today, since current followers of similar ideologies see the world as full of dangerous powers. It is necessary to proclaim to them that Christ is triumphant, so that those who are with Christ, who stay united to him, have nothing and no one to fear. I think that this is also important for us, that we must learn to face all fears because he is above all forms of domination, he is the true Lord of the world.

Even the entire cosmos is subject to him and converges in him as its own head. The words in the Letter to the Ephesians that speak of God's plan "to unite all things in him, things in heaven and things on earth" (1:10) are famous. Likewise, we read in the Letter to the Colossians that "in him all things were created, in heaven and on earth, visible and invisible" (1:16), and that "making peace by the blood of his cross . . . reconcile[d] to himself all things, whether on earth or in heaven" (1:20). Therefore, there is not, on the one hand, the great material world and, on the other, this small reality of the history of our earth, of the world of people: it is all one in Christ. He is the head of the cosmos; the cosmos too was created by him, it was created for us to the extent that we are united with him. It is a rational and personalistic vision of the universe. I would say that it would have been impossible to conceive of a vision more universalistic than this, and that it befits the Risen Christ alone. Christ is the *Pantokrator* ("Ruler of All") to which all things are subordinate. Our thoughts turn precisely to Christ the Pantocrator, who fills the vault of the apse in Byzantine churches, sometimes depicted seated on high, above the whole world, or even on a rainbow, to show his equality with God himself, at whose right hand he is seated (cf. Eph 1:20; Col 3:1), and thus also his incomparable role as the guide of human destiny.

A vision of this kind can only be conceived by the Church, not in the sense that she wishes to misappropriate that to which she is not entitled, but in another double sense: both to the extent that the Church recognizes that Christ is greater than she is, given that his lordship extends beyond her confines, and to the extent that the Church alone, not the cosmos, is described as the Body of Christ. All of this means that we must consider earthly realities positively, since Christ sums them up in himself, and at the same time we must live to the full our specific ecclesial identity, which is the one most homogeneous to Christ's own identity.

Then there is also a special concept which is typical of these two letters, and it is the concept of "mystery." The "mystery of [God's] will" is mentioned once (Eph 1:9) and, other times, as the "mystery of Christ" (Eph 3:4; Col 4:3) or even as "God's mystery, of Christ, in whom are hid all the treasures of wisdom and knowledge" (Col 2:2–3). This refers to God's inscrutable plan for the destiny of mankind, of peoples, and of the world. With this language the two Epistles tell us that the fulfillment of this mystery is found in Christ. If we are with Christ, even if our minds are incapable of grasping everything, we know that we have penetrated the nucleus of this "mystery" and are on the way to the truth. It is he in his totality and not only in one aspect of his Person or at one moment of his existence who bears within him the fullness of the unfathomable divine plan of salvation. In him what is called "the manifold wisdom of God" (Eph 3:10) takes shape, for in him "the whole fulness of deity dwells bodily" (Col 2:9).

From this point on, therefore, it is not possible to reflect on and worship God's will, his sovereign instruction, without comparing ourselves personally with Christ in Person, in whom that "mystery" is incarnate and may be tangibly perceived. Thus one arrives at contemplation of the "unsearchable riches of Christ" (Eph 3:8) which are beyond any human understanding. It is not that God did not leave footprints on his journey, for Christ himself is God's impression, his greatest footprint; but we realize "what is the breadth and length and height and depth" of this mystery "which surpasses knowledge" (Eph 3:18–19). Mere intellectual categories prove inadequate here, and, recognizing that many things are beyond our rational capacities, we must entrust them to the humble and joyful contemplation not only of the mind but also of the heart. The Fathers of the Church, moreover, tell us that love understands better than reason alone.

A last word must be said on the concept, already mentioned above, of the Church as the spousal partner of Christ. In the Second Letter to the Corinthians, the Apostle Paul had compared the Christian community to a bride, writing thus: "I feel a divine jealousy for you, for I betrothed you to Christ to present you as a pure bride to her one husband" (11:2). The Letter to the Ephesians develops this image, explaining that the Church is not only a betrothed bride, but the real bride of Christ. He has won her, so to speak, and has done so at the cost of his life: as the text says, he "gave himself up for her" (Eph 5:25). What demonstration of love could be greater than this? But in addition, he was concerned about her beauty: not only the beauty already acquired through Baptism, but also that beauty "without stain or wrinkle" that is due to an irreproachable life which must grow in her moral conduct every day (cf. Eph 5:26–27).

It is a short step from here to the common experience of Christian marriage; indeed, it is not even very clear what the initial reference point of the letter was for its author: whether it was the Christ-Church relationship, in whose light the union of the man and woman should be seen, or whether it was the experiential event of conjugal union, in whose light should be seen the relationship between Christ and the Church. But both aspects illuminate each other reciprocally: we learn what marriage is in the light of the communion of Christ and the Church, we learn how Christ is united to us in thinking of the mystery of matrimony. In any case, our letter presents itself as nearly a middle road between the prophet Hosea, who expressed the relationship between God and his people in terms of the wedding that had already taken place (cf. Hos 2:4, 16, 20), and the Seer of the Apocalypse, who was to propose the eschatological encounter between the Church and the Lamb as a joyful and indefectible wedding (cf. Rev 19:7–9; 21:9).

There would be much more to say, but it seems to me that from what has been expounded it is already possible to realize that these two letters form a great catechesis, from which we can learn not only how to be good Christians but also how to become truly human. If we begin by understanding that the cosmos is the impression of Christ, we learn our correct relationship with the cosmos, along with all of the problems of the preservation of the cosmos. Let us learn to see it with reason, but with a reason motivated by love, and with the humility and respect that make it possible to act in the right way. And if we believe that the Church is the Body of Christ, that Christ gave himself for her, we learn how to live reciprocal love with Christ, the love that unites us to God and makes us see in the other the image of Christ, Christ himself. Let us pray the Lord to help us to meditate well upon Sacred Scripture, his word, and thus truly learn how to live well.

CHAPTER NINETEEN

Pastoral Epistles:
Letters to Timothy and Titus*

The last of the Pauline letters are known as "pastoral letters," because they were sent to individual pastors of the Church: two to Timothy and one to Titus, both close collaborators of St. Paul. In Timothy, the Apostle saw almost an "alter ego"; in fact he entrusted him with important missions (to Macedonia: cf. Acts 19:22; to Thessalonica: cf. 1 Thess 3:6–7; to Corinth: cf. 1 Cor 4:17; 16:10–11), and then wrote a flattering eulogy on him: "I have no one like him, who will be genuinely anxious for your welfare" (Phil 2:20). According to the *Ecclesiastical History* of Eusebius of Caesarea, a fourth century historian, Timothy was the first Bishop of Ephesus (cf. 3:4). Titus, too, must have been very dear to the Apostle, who explicitly describes him as "earnest in many matters . . . my partner and fellow worker" (2 Cor 8:17–23), and further "my true child in a common faith" (Tit 1:4). He had been assigned a few very delicate missions in the Church of Corinth, whose results heartened Paul (cf. 2 Cor 7:6–7, 13; 8:6). After this, according to the tradition handed down to us, Titus joined Paul in Nicopolis in Epirus, in Greece (cf. Tit 3:12), and was then sent by him to Dalmatia (cf. 2 Tim 4:10). The letter sent to him suggests that he was later made Bishop of Crete (cf. Tit 1:5).

The letters addressed to these two pastors occupy a very particular place within the New Testament. Most exegetes today are

---

* General Audience, January 28, 2009.

of the opinion that these letters would not have been written by Paul himself, but would have come from the "Pauline School," and that they reflect his legacy for a new generation, perhaps including some words or brief passages written by the Apostle himself. Some parts of the Second Letter to Timothy, for example, appear so authentic that they could have come only from the heart and mouth of the Apostle.

Without a doubt, the situation of the Church as it emerges from these letters is very different from that of Paul's middle years. He now, in retrospect, defines himself as the "preacher and apostle, a teacher" of faith and truth to the Gentiles (cf. 1 Tim 2:7; 2 Tim 1:11); he presents himself as one who has received mercy; he writes, "that in me, as the foremost, Jesus Christ might display his perfect patience for an example to those who were to believe in him for eternal life" (1 Tim 1:16). So it is of essential importance that in Paul, a persecutor converted by the presence of the Risen One, the Lord's magnanimity is really shown to encourage us, and lead us to hope and to have faith in the Lord's mercy who, notwithstanding our littleness, can do great things. The new cultural contexts that are assumed here go beyond the middle years of Paul's life. In fact reference is made to the appearance of teachings that must be considered quite erroneous and false (cf. 1 Tim 4:1–2; 2 Tim 3:1–5), such as those [teachings] which held that marriage was not a good thing (cf. 1 Tim 4:3a). We can see a modern equivalent of this worry, because today, too, the Scriptures are sometimes read as an object of historical curiosity and not as the word of the Holy Spirit, in which we can hear the voice of the Lord himself and recognize his presence in history. We could say that, with this brief list of errors presented in the three letters, there are some precocious early traces of that later erroneous movement which goes by the name of Gnosticism (cf. 1 Tim 2:5–6; 2 Tim 3:6–8).

The writer faces these doctrines with two basic reminders. The first consists in an exhortation to a spiritual reading of Sacred Scripture (cf. 2 Tim 3:14–17), that is, to a reading which considers them truly "inspired" and coming from the Holy Spirit, so that one can be "instructed for salvation" by them. The correct way to read the Scriptures is to enter into dialogue with the Holy Spirit, in order to derive a light "for teaching, for reproof, for correction, and for training in righteousness" (2 Tim 3:16). This, the letter adds, is so "that the man of God may be complete, equipped for every good work" (2 Tim 3:17). The other reminder is a reference to the good "deposit" (*parathéke*): a special word found in the pastoral letters and used to indicate the tradition of the apostolic faith which must be safeguarded with the help of the Holy Spirit who dwells in us. This "deposit" is therefore to be considered as the sum of the apostolic Tradition, and as a criterion of faithfulness to the Gospel message.

And here we must bear in mind that the term "Scriptures," when used in the pastoral letters, as in all the rest of the New Testament, means explicitly the Old Testament, since the writings of the New Testament either had not yet been written or did not yet constitute part of the Scriptural canon. Therefore, the Tradition of the apostolic proclamation, this "deposit," is the key to the reading of the Scriptures, the New Testament. In this sense, Scripture and Tradition, Scripture and the apostolic proclamation as a key, are set side by side, and almost merge to form together the "firm foundation laid by God" (cf. 2 Tim 2:19). The apostolic proclamation, that is, Tradition, is necessary in order to enter into an understanding of the Scriptures, and to hear the voice of Christ in them. We must, in fact, "hold firm to the sure word as taught" by the teaching received (Tit 1:9). Indeed, at the basis of everything is faith in the historical revelation of the goodness of God, who in Jesus Christ materially manifested his "loving kindness," a love which in the original Greek text is significantly expressed as *filanthropìa* (Tit 3:4; cf. 2 Tim 1:9–10); God loves humanity.

Altogether, it is clear that the Christian community is beginning to define itself in strict terms, according to an identity which not only stands aloof from incongruous interpretations, but above all affirms its ties to the essential points of faith, which here is synonymous with "truth" (1 Tim 2:4, 7; 4:3; 6:5; 2 Tim 2:15, 18, 25; 3:7–8; 4:4; Tit 1:1, 14). In faith the essential truth of who we are, who God is, and how we must live is made clear. And of this truth (the truth of faith), the Church is described as the "pillar and bulwark" (1 Tim 3:15). In any case, she remains an open community of universal breadth who prays for everyone of every rank and order, so that all may know the truth: God "desires all men to be saved and to come to the knowledge of the truth," because Christ Jesus "gave himself as a ransom for all" (1 Tim 2:4–6). Therefore, the sense of universality, even if the communities are still small, is strong and conclusive in these letters. Furthermore, those in the Christian community "speak evil of no one," and "show perfect courtesy toward all men" (Tit 3:2). This is the first important component of these letters: universality and faith as truth, as a key to the reading of Sacred Scripture, of the Old Testament, thereby defining a unified proclamation of Scripture, a living faith open to all and a witness to God's love for everyone.

Another component typical of these letters is their reflection on the ministerial structure of the Church. They are the first to present the triple subdivision into Bishops, priests, and deacons (cf. 1 Tim 3:1–13; 4:13; 2 Tim 1:6; Tit 1:5–9). We can observe in the pastoral letters the merging of two different ministerial structures, and thus the constitution of the definitive form of the ministry in the Church. In Paul's letters from the middle period of his life, he speaks of "bishops" (Phil 1:1), and of "deacons": this is the typical structure of the Church formed during the time of the Gentile world.

However, as the figure of the Apostle himself remains dominant, the other ministries only slowly develop. If, as we have said, in the Churches formed in the ancient world we have Bishops and deacons, and not priests, in the Churches formed in the Judeo-Christian world, priests are the dominant structure. At the end of the pastoral letters, the two structures unite: now "the bishop" appears (cf. 1 Tim 3:2; Tit 1:7), used always in the singular with the definite article "the bishop." And beside "the bishop" we find priests and deacons. The figure of the Apostle is still prominent, but the three letters, as I have said, are no longer addressed to communities but rather to individuals, to Timothy and Titus, who on the one hand appear as Bishops, and on the other begin to take the place of the Apostle.

This is the first indication of the reality that later would be known as "apostolic succession." Paul says to Timothy in the most solemn tones: "Do not neglect the gift you have, which was given you by prophetic utterance when the elders laid their hands upon you" (1 Tim 4:14). We can say that in these words the sacramental character of the ministry is first made apparent. And so we have the essential Catholic structure: Scripture and Tradition, Scripture and proclamation, form a whole, but to this structure, a doctrinal structure, so to speak, must be added the personal structure, the successors of the Apostles as witnesses to the apostolic proclamation.

Lastly, it is important to note that in these letters, the Church sees herself in very human terms, analogous to the home and the family. Particularly in 1 Tim 3:2–7 we read highly detailed instructions concerning the Bishop, like these: he must be "above reproach, the husband of one wife, temperate, sensible, dignified, hospitable, an apt teacher, no drunkard, not violent but gentle, not quarrelsome, and no lover of money. He must manage his own household well, keeping his children submissive and respectful in every way; for if a man does not know how to manage his own household, how can he care for God's Church? . . . moreover he must be well thought of by outsiders." A special note should be made here of the importance of an aptitude for teaching (cf. also 1 Tim 5:17), which is echoed in other passages (cf. 1 Tim 6:2c; 2 Tim 3:10; Tit 2:1), and also of a special personal characteristic, that of "paternity." In fact the Bishop is considered the father of the Christian community (cf. also 1 Tim 3:15). For that matter, the idea of the Church as "the Household of God" is rooted in the Old Testament (cf. Num 12:7) and is repeated in Heb 3:2, 6, while elsewhere we read that all Christians are no longer strangers or guests, but fellow citizens of the saints and members of the household of God (cf. Eph 2:19).

Let us ask the Lord and St. Paul that we too, as Christians, may be ever more characterized, in relation to the society in which we live, as members of the "family of God." And we pray that the pastors of the Church may increasingly acquire paternal sentiments tender and at the same time strong in the formation of the House of God, of the community, and of the Church.

CHAPTER TWENTY

St. Paul's Life and Legacy[*]

At the conclusion of our catecheses on St. Paul we shall speak of the end of his earthly life. The ancient Christian tradition witnesses unanimously that Paul died as a consequence of his martyrdom here in Rome. The New Testament writings tell us nothing of the event. The Acts of the Apostles end their account by mentioning the imprisonment of the Apostle, who was nevertheless able to welcome all who went to him (cf. Acts 28:30–31). Only in the Second Letter to Timothy do we find these premonitory words: "For I am already on the point of being sacrificed; the time of my departure has come" (2 Tim 4:6; cf. Phil 2:17). Two images are used here, the religious image of sacrifice that he had used previously in the Letter to the Philippians, interpreting martyrdom as a part of Christ's sacrifice, and the nautical image of casting off: two images which together discreetly allude to the event of death and of a brutal death.

The first explicit testimony of St. Paul's death comes to us from the middle of the 90s in the first century, thus more than three decades after his actual death. It consists precisely in the epistle that the Church of Rome, with its Bishop Clement I, wrote to the Church of Corinth. In that epistolary text is an invitation to keep her eyes fixed on the example of the Apostles and, immediately after the mention of Peter's martyrdom, one reads: "Owing to envy, Paul also obtained the reward of patient endurance, after being seven times thrown into captivity, compelled to

---

* General Audience, February 4, 2009.

flee, and stoned. After preaching both in the east and the west, he gained the illustrious reputation due to his faith, having taught righteousness to the whole world, and come to the extreme limit of the west, and suffered martyrdom under the prefects. Thus was he removed from the world, and went into a holy place, having proved himself a striking example of patience" (*1 Clem* 5:2). The patience of which Clement speaks is an expression of Paul's communion with the Passion of Christ, of the generosity and constancy with which he accepted a long journey of suffering so as to be able to say, "I bear on my body the marks of Jesus" (Gal 6:17). In St. Clement's text we heard that Paul had arrived at the "extreme limit of the west." Whether this is a reference to a voyage in Spain undertaken by Paul is open to discussion. There is no certainty on it, but it is true that in his Letter to the Romans St. Paul expresses his intention to go to Spain (cf. Rom 15:24).

The sequence in Clement's letter of the two names of Peter and Paul is, however, very interesting, even if they were to be inverted in the testimony of Eusebius of Caesarea in the fourth century. Referring to the Emperor Nero, Eusebius was to write: "It is, therefore, recorded that Paul was beheaded in Rome itself, and that Peter likewise was crucified during Nero's reign. This account is substantiated by the fact that their names are preserved in the cemetery of that place even to the present day" (*Ecclesiastical History,* 2, 25, 5). Eusebius then goes on to reference the earlier declaration of a Roman priest named Gaius that dates back to the early second century: "I can show the trophies of the Apostles. For if you go to the Vatican or on the Ostian Way, you will find the trophies of those who laid the foundations of this Church" (ibid., 2, 25, 6–7). "Trophies" are sepulchral monuments; these were the actual tombs of Peter and Paul which we still venerate today, after 2,000 years, in those same places: that of St. Peter here in the Vatican and that of the Apostle to the Gentiles in the Basilica of St. Paul Outside the Walls on the Ostian Way.

It is interesting to note that the two great Apostles are mentioned together. Although no ancient source speaks of a contemporary ministry of both in Rome, subsequent Christian knowledge, on the basis of their common burial in the capital of the Empire, was also to associate them as founders of the Church of Rome. In fact this can be read in Irenaeus of Lyons, toward the end of the second century, concerning apostolic succession in the various Churches: "Since, however, it would be very tedious, in such a volume as this, to reckon up the successions of all the Churches . . . [we do this] by indicating that tradition derived from the apostles, of the very great, the very ancient, and universally known Church founded and organized at Rome by the two most glorious Apostles, Peter and Paul" (*Adversus Haereses,* 3, 3, 2).

However, let us now set Peter aside and concentrate on Paul. His martyrdom is recounted for the first time in the *Acts of Paul,* written towards the end of the second century. They say that Nero condemned him to death by beheading, an order which was carried out immediately (cf. 9:5). The date of his death already varies in the ancient sources which set it between the persecution unleashed by Nero himself after the burning of Rome in July 64 and the last year of his reign, that is, the year 68 (cf. Jerome, *De viris ill.* 5, 8). The calculation heavily depends on the chronology of Paul's arrival in Rome, a discussion into which we cannot enter here. Later traditions specify two other elements. One, the most legendary, is that his martyrdom occurred at the *Acquae Salviae,* on the *Via Laurentina*, and that his head rebounded three times, giving rise to a source of water each time that it touched the ground, which is why, to this day, the place is called the "*Tre Fontane*" [three fountains] (*Acts of Peter and Paul by the Pseudo-Marcellus,* fifth century). The second version, in harmony with the ancient account of the priest Gaius mentioned above, is that his burial not only took place "outside the city . . . at the second mile on the Ostian Way," but more precisely "on the estate of

Lucina," who was a Christian matron (*Passion of Paul by the Pseudo-Abdias,* fourth century). It was here, in the fourth century, that the Emperor Constantine built a first church. Then, between the fourth and fifth centuries it was considerably enlarged by the Emperors Valentinian II, Theodosius, and Arcadius. The present-day Basilica of St. Paul Outside the Walls was built here after the fire in 1800.

In any case, the figure of St. Paul towers far above his earthly life and his death; in fact, he left us an extraordinary spiritual heritage. He too, as a true disciple of Christ, became a sign of contradiction. While he was considered apostate by Mosaic law among the "Ebionites," a Judeo-Christian group, great veneration for St. Paul already appears in the Acts of the Apostles. I would now like to prescind from the apocryphal literature, such as the *Acts of Paul and Thekla* and an apocryphal collection of letters between the Apostle Paul and the philosopher Seneca. It is above all important to note that St. Paul's letters very soon entered the liturgy, where the structure Prophet-Apostle-Gospel is crucial for the form of the Liturgy of the Word. Thus, thanks to this "presence" in the Church's liturgy, the Apostle's thought immediately gave spiritual nourishment to the faithful of every epoch.

It is obvious that the Fathers of the Church, and subsequently all theologians, were nourished by the letters of St. Paul and by his spirituality. Thus he has remained throughout the centuries and up to this day the true teacher and Apostle to the Gentiles. The first patristic comment on a New Testament text that has come down to us is that of the great Alexandrian theologian, Origen, who comments on Paul's Letter to the Romans. Unfortunately, only part of this comment is extant. St. John Chrysostom, in addition to commenting on Paul's letters, wrote seven memorable *Panegyrics* (sermons) on him. It was to Paul that St. Augustine owed the crucial step of his own conversion, and to Paul that he returned throughout his life. His great Catholic theology derives from this ongoing dialogue with the Apostle, as does the Protestant theology in every age. St. Thomas Aquinas has left us a beautiful comment on the Pauline letters, which represents the ripest fruit of medieval exegesis.·

A true turning point was reached in the 16th century with the Protestant Reformation. The decisive moment in Luther's life was the "Turmerlebnis" (1517), the moment in which he discovered a new interpretation of the Pauline doctrine of justification. It was an interpretation that freed him from the scruples and anxieties of his previous life and gave him a new radical trust in the goodness of God who forgives all, unconditionally. From that time Luther identified Judeo-Christian legalism, condemned by the Apostle, with the order of life of the Catholic Church. And the Church therefore appeared to him as an expression of the slavery of the law which he countered with the freedom of the Gospel. The Council of Trent, from 1545 to 1563, profoundly interpreted the question of justification and found the synthesis between law and Gospel to be in line with the entire Catholic tradition, in conformity with the message of Sacred Scripture read in its totality and unity.

The 19th century, gathering the best heritage of the Enlightenment, underwent a new revival of Paulinism, now developed by the historical-critical interpretation of Sacred Scripture, above all at the level of scientific work. Here we shall prescind from the fact that even in that century, as later in the 20th century, a true and proper denigration of St. Paul emerged. I am thinking primarily of Nietzsche, who derided the theology of St. Paul's humility, opposing it with his theology of the strong and powerful man. However, let us set this aside and examine the essential current of the new scientific interpretation of Sacred Scripture and of the new Paulinism of that century. Here, the concept of freedom has been emphasized as central to Pauline thought; in it was found the heart of Pauline thought, as Luther, moreover, had already intuited. Yet the concept of freedom was then reinterpreted in the context of modern liberalism. The differentiation between the proclamation of St. Paul and the proclamation of Jesus was thus heavily emphasized. And St. Paul appears almost as a new founder of Christianity.

It is true that in St. Paul the centrality of the Kingdom of God, crucial for the proclamation of Jesus, was transformed into the centrality of Christology, whose crucial point is the Paschal Mystery. And it is from the Paschal Mystery that the Sacraments of Baptism and of the Eucharist derive, as a permanent presence of this mystery from which the Body of Christ grows and the Church is built. However, I would say, without going into detail here, that precisely in the new centrality of Christology, and of the Paschal Mystery, the Kingdom of God is realized and the authentic proclamation of Jesus becomes concrete, present, and active. We have seen in our previous Catecheses that this Pauline innovation is truly the deepest fidelity to the proclamation of Jesus. In the progress of exegesis, especially in the past 200 years, the points of convergence between Catholic exegesis and Protestant exegesis have increased, thereby achieving a notable consensus precisely on the point that was the origin of the greatest historical dissent. There is thus great hope for the cause of ecumenism, so central to the Second Vatican Council.

Finally, I would like to mention briefly the various religious movements named after St. Paul that have come into being in the Catholic Church in modern times. This happened in the 16th century with the "Congregation of St. Paul," known as the Barnabites; in the 19th century with the "Missionaries of St. Paul," or Paulist Fathers; in the 20th century with the polyform "Pauline Family" founded by Bl. Giacomo Alberione, not to mention of the secular institute of the "Company of St. Paul." Essentially, we still have before us the luminous figure of an Apostle and of an extremely fruitful and profound Christian thinker, from whose approach everyone can benefit. In one of his panegyrics, St. John Chrysostom established an original comparison between Paul and Noah. He says: Paul "did not put beams together to build an ark; rather, instead of joining planks of wood he wrote letters and thus rescues from the billows not two, three, or five members of his own family but the entire ecumene that was on the point of perishing" (*Paneg.* 1, 5). The Apostle Paul can still and will always be able to do exactly that. Drawing from him as much from his example as from his doctrine will therefore be an incentive, if not a guarantee, for the reinforcement of the Christian identity of each one of us and for the rejuvenation of the entire Church.